Raising
Interfaith
Children

Raising
Interfaith
Children

Spiritual Orphans

or Spiritual Heirs?

Donna E. Schaper

A Crossroad Book
The Crossroad Publishing Company
New York

The Crossroad Publishing Company
370 Lexington Avenue, New York, NY 10017

Printed in the United States of America

Library of Congress Cataloging-in-Publication Data
Schaper, Donna.
    Raising interfaith children : spiritual orphans or spiritual heirs? /
by Donna E. Schaper.
       p.   cm.
    Includes bibliographical references (p.).
    ISBN 0-8245-1632-X (pbk.)
    1. Interfaith marriage – United States. 2. Children of interfaith
marriage – United States. 3. Parenting – Religious aspects – Judaism.
4. Parenting – Religious aspects – Christianity. I. Title.
HQ1031.S28   1999
306.84'3'0973 – DC21   99-12785

1   2   3   4   5   6   7   8   9   10   04   03   02   01   00   99

Contents

Glossary

Baptism: A ritual using water as a sign to initiate a child into the church in the name of the Trinitarian God, traditionally, for children, at seven days after birth, but now more normally any time during the first year.

Bar/Bat Mitzvah: The rite of passage to become a son (Bar) or daughter (Bat) of the Commandments, usually at the onset of adolescence, or about age thirteen. One becomes a full-fledged member of the Jewish community and is obligated to perform the commandments.

Bimah: A platform in a synagogue holding the reading table used when chanting or reading portions of the Torah and the Prophets.

B'Nai Mitzvah: Children of the Commandments. We had twins, a girl and a boy, who together celebrated their Bar and Bat Mitzvah. Thus our use of this relatively uncommon term.

Brit: A covenant or pledge of obligation between two parties that hearkens back to the three pledges God made with the Jewish people: the Shabbat, the rainbow, and the circumcision. Usually made eight days after the birth of a child. Also, the rite of circumcision.

Chanukah, or Hanukkah: A minor Jewish festival celebrated in December to remember the Maccabeans and their fight for liberty and to commemorate the miracle of the light. Often paired with Christmas, which is a major Christian festival.

Christmas: Christian celebration of the traditional day of the birth of Jesus Christ, December 25.

Chutzpah: A Yiddish word meaning gutsiness or forcefulness.

Confirmation: The rite of passage of Christian adolescence into full membership in the congregation.

Daven: To recite the prescribed prayers in a Jewish liturgy.

Dreidel: A four-sided top bearing Hebrew letters on each side, used chiefly in a children's game traditionally played on the Jewish festival of Hanukkah.

Easter: Celebrated by Christians as the day that Christ rose from the dead. Observed in the spring the first Sunday after the first full moon after the vernal equinox.

First and Second Testaments: Terms used by increasing numbers of interfaith and multifaith people to refer to the "Old Testament" and the "New Testament." Jews observe only the first and Christians observe both.

Generativity: Term used by psychoanalyst Erik Erikson to mean maturity, or the capacity to give back to the world.

Goy (pl., Goyim): A non-Jewish person; a Gentile. Sometimes used disparagingly.

Hirosis: Apple-walnut-wine dish on the Passover plate; symbolizes the mortar of the bricks made by the Jews when they were slaves in Egypt.

Interfaith: More than one faith, blended faiths. Often substituted for "multifaith."

Jesus: A Jew who for Christians is the long-awaited Messiah.

L'Chaim: "To life," a common Jewish blessing.

Menorah: The nine-candle candelabra used at Chanukah. Each night one additional candle is lit by the "Shama," the lead candle, to commemorate the Maccabeans.

Multifaith: Describes relationship in which the integrity of each traditional faith remains coherent while relating to another faith. Often very hard to distinguish between interfaith and multifaith.

Passover: A Jewish holiday beginning on the fourteenth of Nisan and commemorating the Hebrews' liberation from slavery in Egypt.

Seder: The Passover meal during which the Exodus from Egypt is recalled.

Shabbat, or Sabbath: The day of rest, beginning as all Jewish days do the night before. Instituted as part of the covenant between God and the people in Exodus 31:16–17. Practiced by Jews on Friday night and Saturday, by Christians on Sunday.

Tithe: The Jewish and Christian practice, ordained by God in the First Testament, of giving back one-tenth of the fruits of our labor.

Yarmulke: A skullcap worn especially by Orthodox or Conservative Jewish males in the synagogue and the home.

Yom Kippur: a Jewish high holy day observed on the tenth day of the month of Tishri by abstinence from food and drink and by the day-long recitation of prayers of repentance in the synagogue. Also called Day of Atonement.

Fiddlers on the Roof

When I fell in love with Warren Goldstein almost two decades ago, I moved to another town, hoping the matter would disappear before I'd have to make a decision about him. What bothered me most was how little his faith disturbed me. I couldn't find a spiritual reason not to marry him; I could find a host of practical ones, including the fact that I might not get any more jobs in the church that I love and that my children might be mixed up. These two muscular reasons told me not to enter into an interfaith marriage. But when I spoke with my God in the way that I do — as a friend, viscerally, sometimes too familiarly as "my Maker" — God never peeped. God never said no. God always whispered, gently, why not? After hours of consultations with fellow clergy, therapists, friends, books, ghosts, and family, I decided to marry Warren.

I had many new questions about God and faith traditions, Jews and Christians, Jesus and Israel — and on and on. Here I answer a few of these questions. Here I give a spiritual account for our decision to marry and our decision to raise our children "both ways," fully Jewish and fully Christian. I choose an "interfaith" approach, meaning a blend. Warren is more comfortable with "multifaith," main-

taining the distinctions. We do not agree; rather, we raise
our children both ways: Jewish and Christian, interfaith and
multifaith.

The account is not so much theological as spiritual, not
so much a defense as a story, not so much an argument as a
probing. Here we have religious identity as constructed from
"below." I have tried to be in faithful dialogue with both traditions, but I have not used their answers. I have used ours.
There are some pretty big differences between Warren and
me, and lots of religion is lost along the way — even while
God is often more present than rabbis, priests, and clergy
know. As one friend of mine from Israel puts it, religion is
too important to let the rabbis manage it. The same goes
for ordained clergy. Organized religion could have been more
helpful to us; it was not. But that did not prohibit God from
partnering with us.

I have staked my children's souls on what I know to be
true, not what is right. That should tell you some of my
affection for the former and my suspicion of the latter. I
am a part of a little movement in the church called "Saving
Jesus from Those Who Are Right." I hope to save my three
children from those who are right about religion.

Isaac Eugene (named for the socialist Eugene Debs) Goldstein was a Bar Mitzvah in 1996, along with thousands of
other people's children. While I love their stories, I want
to tell you mine. Isaac's Jewish grandparents lived all over
the world in mobile military style: his grandmother drove
his father forty-five minutes each way, twice a week, to Hebrew School. His Christian grandparents worked for Jews in
the garment industry all their lives. One fired his Christian
grandfather at age sixty, so as not to pay a pension.

The interfaith life is a life of extras, both in payments and
in gifts. We always have double the heritage that anyone else

has. Our kids would be the first to tell you what it is like to go to Christian Sunday School and Jewish Sunday School.

Isaac's father is a Jewish professor of American history. Formerly agnostic, he is now enthusiastic about his Judaism. Isaac converted him when he read from the Torah. The rabbi and the steward of the text pointed to the wrong place in the text. Isaac gently corrected them, not just in public but in front of his father. "No," said he. "That is not my portion." Much hub-bub. Sure enough, it was not his portion. His portion was further down in the text.

Because of my profession and the fact that we had agreed to an early immersion in Christian Sunday School, through Bar and Bat Mitzvah age, I had simply assumed that the children would choose Christianity. Before Warren's heart converted, I was the only believer around. Now that he has found God, I have trouble. My children may not choose my faith.

Isaac's siblings, eighteen months younger, are twins, Jacob Frederick (named for abolitionist Frederick Douglass) and Katie Emma (named for anarchist Emma Goldman). We agreed on biblical names for both Jacob and Isaac, but we could not bring ourselves to ancient texts for our daughter. She is named for Katharine Hepburn. We have often slid out of our differences through culture, or poetry, or history, or humor. These transcend religion in ways that religions don't know how to transcend themselves. Yet.

We also have a large common faith in God's partnership in social transformation, God's genuine intention to distribute all the wealth and power around. Thus, our children's middle names are as important as their first names. If we did not have such strong and common faith in the justice of God, more of the interfaith particulars would probably be more troublesome than they are. A religious crisis in our interfaith home is as apt to be a boy wanting a gun as an interpretation of a text.

At this moment my three teenage children all appear to be deciding to be "Jewish" and are leaving me stranded in my religious vocation. Their names are, after all, Isaac Goldstein, Jacob Goldstein, and Katie Goldstein. (I have kept my first husband's name.)

What does this mixture feel like to me? It feels like what Jews feel all the time, every day. I am getting the experience of being a minority, and I don't like it one bit.

The kids are right about the Bar and Bat Mitzvah being a better party than Confirmation. One friend suggested a "Confirmitzvah." Marian Wright Edelman celebrated a "Baptist Bar Mitzvah" at each son's coming of age.[1] Her Jewish husband and she celebrated with a ritual presided over by a rabbi and Mrs. Edelman's brother, the Reverend Harry S. Wright. Some two hundred friends, relatives, and neighbors crowded into the Edelmans' large backyard in northwest Washington for the festive occasion. On the other hand, we chose to have a completely Jewish Bar/Bat Mitzvah for each child and a completely Christian Confirmation.

For Isaac's party, we roasted a lamb in the back yard. Nancy, a Buddhist-leaning Christian who lives with us, made twelve homemade rhubarb cakes from the garden. I had Isaac's birth certificate blown up and made a big display of all his childhood trophies and report cards. Eighty people came. The children played baseball; the adults wept. After the big day of his coming of age, I joined the weepers, the ones whose tears tell them time is passing. I spent days singing from Peter Pan. I wasn't crooning for Isaac.

Songs and culture carried what religion could not. His maturity is much more important to me than his faith; his maturing, actively, daily, almost a new child every morning now, is more important to me than what he is at any given moment. I have had days upon days of seeing my son and glimpsing his future. The tears were also tears of joy.

Even if I have become religiously small, I don't want my children to grow up that way. That he exists, is, is created: this is my joy. White roses smelled through the bedroom the day we brought him home from the hospital; they were out again for the Bar Mitzvah. That smell matters. It comes, and it comes again. For me that joy goes deeper spiritually than any of my creeds or contexts.

When Katie and Jacob celebrated their B'Nai Mitzvah this past summer, I focused on the word "thrive." I remembered the day Warren and I saw the two eggs developing in my womb through the sonogram. I was thirty-eight years old — and had the laugh of Sarah about the whole thing. To imagine those two tall, slim, gorgeous, tanned children standing at the Bimah after coming from those little companion eggs took only one word: "thrive." To thank God that they have thrived. That they were sons and daughters of the Torah was magnificent — but that they were alive was even more so. (Especially since we had to wean Jacob off twenty-six tubes and sing Easter hymns to him in an infant intensive care unit!) They thrive. That's the spiritual content of the matter. All the rest is "commentary." All the rest is more like poetry.

When I get beyond wanting to control my children's religious futures, which I do want to control but know I cannot, I go to a deeper religious place, where real is real, where rose is rose. Where God is near. So go my theological hopes for my children — maturity, growth, and a place to worship God. A place to get broken, a place to get healed. A white rose come, a white rose gone, a white rose come again.

In her poem "Kyrie," Ellen Bryant Voigt asks the question "When does a childhood end? . . . the boys still on the playground / routing evil with their little sticks." I identify so with those little boys! I am defending awesome mystery with a little stick of particularity. Yes, it is mine. But it is so small.

At the end of Isaac's party, the Bar Mitzvah boy played "Take Me Out to the Ball Game" on his saxophone — and we all tried to get home, a place we left when we married "across" lines.

I may be most interested in my children's stories, but I know they are not the only stories. We lived next door to a couple from Teheran. She is Jewish; he is Moslem. They too raise their children both ways. On the night of the famous handshake in Israel — when we all thought peace was on its way — I was standing in Arlene's living room. We were deciding who would pick up our kids up from basketball practice. As we saw the hands shake, tears came into the eyes of both of us. We held hands in a ceremony of the kitchen. One of the kids said, "Guys, it's just a basketball game. We don't care that much who wins." Their misunderstanding was pure Spirit — our tears were also.

Blending is increasing. I am part of that increase. A few facts will give context to the poetry and the particulars I tell in this book. In a *Newsweek* story we learn that the proportion of Jews who married Gentiles, around one in ten for the first half of the twentieth century, according to the American Jewish Committee, doubled by 1960, doubled again by the early 1970s, and in the 1990s leveled off at just over 50 percent.[2] To put it another way, by some estimates one out of three American Jews lives in an interfaith family. In a 1990 survey cited by psychologist Joel Crohn, an authority on mixed marriages, the rates are 21 percent for Catholics, 30 percent for Mormons, and 40 percent for Muslims. We don't really have good figures on how many convert, how many go completely secular, or how many go "both ways." Gabrielle Glaser, who studies intermarriage in her book *Strangers to the Tribe,* argues that "a significant number of Jews who marry outside their faith are making serious efforts to pass on the religion and culture of their forefathers. If the interfaith couples I met," says she, "over the past few years are any measure [Judaism] will surely survive modern intermarriage."[3]

In *The Intermarriage Handbook* Judy Petsonk and Jim Remsen provide dozens of stories about the way different people have handled different differences.[4] They tell the story of Pareveh, the Alliance for Adult Children of Jewish-Gentile Intermarriage, which is a national support group for people who have a hard time being intermarried. They argue that there are four choices facing interfaith parents when it comes to raising children: they can raise them in one culture, to which the other parent may or may not convert; they can raise them conscientiously in both cultures; they can select a third culture; or they can raise them with no particular religious or cultural traditions at all.[5] I might add a fifth option, which I see every now and then, which is to combine these different choices developmentally. Parents can also choose one strategy for one life moment and another for another.

I was at a worship service where the text was "We worship the God from whom every family in heaven and on earth takes its name" (Eph. 3:15). I nearly died. Here I was just beginning to manage the words "interfaith," "intrafaith," and "conversion," and here was ancient scripture advocating a puzzling unity. How could the Rosenbaums' wonderful harmonized Jewish/Christian calendar, replete with menus, coexist with this text?[6] Was a handshake possible?

Obviously, I think so. I believe God can be more than humans can understand about God. I believe cultures help religion tell its story. How? Why? What is my authority?

First it is my experience. And second it is the tension of Tevya in *Fiddler on the Roof,* whose daughter falls in love with a man who is not Jewish. He and I are comrades — and we are comrades with lots of other parents whose experience of letting children go to a place they can't quite see is very similar. We don't need interfaith marriage to have a problem letting our children go into the future. (My Isaac swears he is going to outer space.)

Another authority is a woman I met for only a few minutes at an apartment wedding in Philadelphia. I had been asked to perform the ceremony. It was interfaith, but no rabbi would come near, back then, in the early seventies. Reports were everywhere not only that the grandmother was going to die rather than see the service continue but that she was also disinheriting the lot. When she arrived a few minutes before the service, she took her dignified seat in the front row. Then, cane and head held high, she turned around to the small crowd and said, "Mazel Tov." The tears began. How many times as a pastor I have seen this very occurrence. Over and over again, grandmothers negate only to affirm. What, anyway, are their choices? Because they can affirm, I can affirm. One of the ways we mixed-up types manage the difficulty of diversity's collision with unity is by remembering with Susan Schneider that "endogamy isn't easy either."[7]

My lightness about intermarriage is not meant to offend those who find the subject difficult. I am not advocating my position so much as expressing it. One rabbi told me just this summer that she simply finds it "impossible" that children could be raised "both ways." My attitude is not insensitive to these difficulties; rather, my point of view is anti-general in general. I don't believe we can claim to speak for the religious experience of other people. In that humility lies my confidence. Mine is just one story.

There are plenty of good books on the generalized story. Consider *Who Is a Jew? Conversations, Not Conclusions* by Meryl Hyman.[8] The phrase "mixed blessings" is used everywhere in the literature, and it is not just a cliché. Nathan Glaser has some hard things to say about Jews who are accused of not providing good leadership during the Holocaust; quite negatively, he compares the failure to work with the issues of intermarriage to the failure of leadership in the Holocaust.[9]

Institutions as well as books approach the issue of intermarriage. All the major and minor branches of Judaism have special commissions and conferences on intermarriage. Margaret Clark of the progressive Jewish Reconstructionist Federation struggles with the role Gentile members should play. The federation is considered American Judaism's smallest but fastest-growing branch with ninety Reconstructionist congregations. The movement, based in Wyncote, Pennsylvania, treats men and women equally in religious practice and welcomes homosexual couples and interfaith families. Called "open and accepting" congregations, they are similar to many Christian congregations that welcome the participation of Jews.

The Reform movement had began to reach out to such couples long ago. Still, every community needs boundaries, even a liberal community, and these communities are in deep, populist dialogue among their own members about how to relate. Simultaneously, religious congregations are being advised to "niche" themselves well to gain adherents. Thus, lax boundaries compete with institutional self-interest.

The core issue in these institutional matters is that non-Jews are raising Jewish or multifaith or interfaith or Christian children anyway, with or without institutional support. According to a Philadelphia-based AP story on July 11,

1998, interfaith families raise their children as Jews in the same proportion as single-faith families do.

Adding to the institutional enigma, there are nagging philosophical issues. John Hick says, "Either there is some support for our being, a fixed foundation for our knowledge, or we cannot escape the forces of darkness that envelop us with madness, with intellectual and moral chaos."[10]

We pluralists beg off these "big" issues on behalf of our experience. We are, as someone said of the journalist Murray Kempton, "interested in everything and nothing else." We believe in things that drive philosophers appropriately mad — that as pluralists, we are people who imagine we can have it both ways. We are rightly and often accused of the cheap pluralism of J. Rich clothing's "Don't Passover our Easter Ties." Or of the ridicule intended in political cartoons showing two rabbis and a Santa, representing Orthodox, Conservative, and Reform Judaism. We are indeed guilty of putting things together that may not appropriately relate. But we are not guilty of denying relationship and interesting possibilities.

The core issue is that non-Jews *are* raising Jewish children. I'd bet our farm on Warren's children not being raised Jewish had he married a Jew. Religion often gets more attention in an intermarriage than it does in an unmixed marriage, where a lot is taken for granted.

A wide assortment of good, practical advice is given for children of intermarriage. In summary, the advice is that children imitate their parents' courage and find their own way to God.[11]

There are lots of clichés developing about American tumbleweeds, or spiritual orphans, or mingled roots, or mixed blessings. There are also literary writers tackling the subject. John Houseman, born in 1902 of a British mother

and an Alsatian Jewish father, wrote a theater memoir entitled "The Education of a Chameleon." A cartoon of a
four-year-old boy in an elevator says, "I'm half Jewish and
half nothing." For me art and humor tell more than the so-
ciology and the statistics — but experience alone is such a
fragile hook on which to hang one's hat that other people's
well-understood experience becomes terribly important to
interfaith pioneers.

There are many people who say, "You can't do this." To
these people we say, "Deal with the real world," which is
what Steve and Cokie Roberts said this last Easter when they
shared the Seder to honor his Jewish faith and went to Easter
Mass because she is Catholic. We don't need to say "deal" in
a hostile manner; we need to say it gently. But "dealing" is
what we are doing.

Because so much attention is given to the problem of Jewish survival, in the light of the Holocaust, Christians often
are quite inarticulate about our concerns with intermarriage.
Obviously, Jews have one problem, which is survival, and
Protestants another with intermarriage. Our problem is that
of fuzzy borders. As Robert McAfee Brown puts it, Protestantism "is all over the place. It does not have recognizable
boundaries; it is extremely difficult to know when an individual or a church has ceased to become Protestant."[12]

In *One Jesus, Many Christs: How Jesus Inspired Not One
True Christianity but Many,* by Gregory J. Riley,[13] we discover that the fuzzy borders of Christianity came in the very
beginning of the faith. Even the early church didn't agree on
the relationship of Jesus to Judaism. The two faiths do have
parallel histories; there is no Christianity without Judaism.
From the very beginning, both faiths have known the tension
between universalism and radical relativism; both have wondered if there is anything but a chasm between the two. I live

in what others call the chasm. But I don't see it as a chasm at all. This problem of the connection of the two faiths is probably best addressed by children raised in both traditions. Surely, they will become more like Jesus, who after all was raised a Jew. Maybe interfaith grandchildren will have a new perspective on an ancient difficulty.

I still think *Fiddler on the Roof* has the right approach to interfaith marriage. We must sing Tevya's song of tension: wail for tradition and follow the children to the canopy. What is a family anyway if not a blend of tradition and adventure? Past and future? I know the sociological definition, that "families are understood to be persons bound together by blood ties or mutual commitments that are sustained by shared memory and common hope." It is a good textbook definition. But families are also root and wing, earth and sky, now and then.

As our hybrid seeds begin to grow, I have discovered at least nine sites of interest and difficulty. They constitute the chapters of this account. Chapter 1 is about origins and destinations and what happens when they fly far apart. Chapter 2 is about rights and rites and how interfaith families raising children both ways use the liturgies available to them. Chapter 3 is about fundamentalism, which is a real threat to interfaith living. Chapter 4 is about foundations, which are as important a friend as fundamentalism is an enemy; we are anti-fundamentalism and pro-foundations. Chapter 5 is about religious authority, which is a very dangerous and rich subject for interfaith people. Chapter 6 is about institutional lag, the way institutions are terribly far behind people in understanding God right now. (It is impossible to say how deeply scarred Jews can be when a rabbi refuses to marry them in an interfaith setting. This rejection often turns them away from the synagogue.) Chapter 7 is about the peculiar kind of conflict that interfaith living is. We can be very positive about our choices and still have lots of conflict around them. Chapter 8 is about monotheism, which is another major problem for interfaith living. And chapter 9 is a letter to my grandchildren, which sums up the hopes that survive the fears stated in the book.

In his biographies of Gandhi and Luther, Erik Erikson said that both were leaders because of the way they embodied the conflicts of their time. If I am a leader in my church, it is because of the conflicts I embody. God brings me to a chasm to live. I don't live there alone but with God and with spiritual orphans whose inheritance I wager my life on.

Chapter One

Nests within Nests

We interfaith families are often the way we are because we can't be the way we were. We are reluctant pilgrims. We haven't flown the coop or destroyed the nest so much as gone deeper inside it. We are not trying to destroy religious tradition so much as to make it honest to contemporary experience. Are we better than other people who stay "home"? No. Nor are we worse.

We married out of the tribe. By "tribe" I do not mean something negative as compared to something modern and progressive. I do not mean that primitive or simplistic sense of tribe but rather root, source, original. We married and bred outside the previously normal way. We married outside of our religious tree, Protestant to Catholic, or Jew to Moslem, or any other combination. Some scholars estimate that as many as one-third of Americans are "interfaith" in the sense that they married outside their original faith.

Interfaith families move backward and forward at the same time. We are going back to an original human religious unity, an imagined if not actual Eden, and forward to something unknown. We build a nest as we go. That nest takes twigs from the past and the future — and sometimes doesn't house us at all.

Interfaith families incorporate a range of tribes. We no

longer come from just one place. We are originals. Very few world cultures have blended to the degree that we Americans blend: most remain against religious blending because it is culturally "impure" and "diluted." These blends may be impure, but they are certainly not diluted. We are becoming phenomenally rich, perhaps even concentrated. The wealth we know is directly the result of our religious traditions: they gave us the strength for homelessness. They permit wilderness and Exodus — and sometimes even encourage it.

Our wealth is not without problems. Not all hybrids work or even survive. We are sometimes stranded. We don't really know that our children will repeat us in that comforting way that they are supposed to. Which God will the children of religiously blended families worship? No one knows or can know. Will the God they choose confirm one parent over against the other? Perhaps not, but along the way there will be plenty of overt and covert competition for the progeny.

Despite the fact that most parents in interfaith families have made a decision for spiritual blend, they may still want their children on "their side." When Philip Roth won the Pulitzer Prize, Leslie Fiedler said of him that he is "ferociously ambivalent....That's what I like about him."[14] The same is true of interfaith families: we are ferociously ambivalent. On our surface, we argue cultural blend. Deep inside, we often march to the instructions of our cultural tribe. We are a transitional people: we dance the new dances and the old dances in a new step. Dancers tell us that the beauty of the dance comes in the transitional moments: thus the wealth and the risk of interfaith dancing.

Some of us in blended families have been advised that we will not cross the Jordan. We won't know what the new land will be like or whether our blended children will speak the name of Yahweh or Jesus or Allah. Or, God forbid, no name.

We interfaith families live in a strangely parochial world: our choice for blend places us in a quiet minority. We have stirred things up religiously, much more than any of us ever imagined we would. We have stirred up our families, for sure, but we have also stirred up an inner dialogue with ourselves about God. Is God many or is God one? Is God ours or theirs, or ours and theirs, or is God beyond the captivity of any of us? Who is God if God is not what we grew up thinking God was?

One of my favorite ways of imagining God is to use the text of Deuteronomy 32:11, where Moses sings that "the eagle stirs its nest." God is imagined as an eagle who leads the people from on high. This verse is immortalized in the Alma Mater of Tougaloo College as written by Jonathan Henderson:

> Tougaloo, Eagle Queen, we love thee:
> Mother Eagle, Stir the nest
> Rout thine eaglets to the breezes:
> They enjoy the test.

Interfaith families are enjoying the test some of the time. We too are led by God, but it is probably not the God Moses was singing about. This God is not saving only us or our tribe: this God is soaring above and out ahead of humanity. In many contexts the Christian gospels say that Jesus "went ahead of them." Interfaith families join God in flight: we fly between origin and destination in unusual ways. All human beings make that flight: our instructions are to find a new flight pattern.

The baby bird that doesn't fly doesn't achieve full maturity. It stays stuck in the nest — for fear of the beyond. Interfaith families are spiritual refugees: we have left the old land, are on our way to the new land, and are not sure that we are going to get to the other side. We identify a great deal with genuine refugees. We say things we don't quite believe, like "It's the same God." And we believe things that no one else really believes, like "It's the same God." The answer to the question about whose God represents religious universalism is usually the impossible "both." No, that is not a Yiddish joke. It is what we, who are ferociously ambivalent, think.

I think of a girl from Zaire who spoke on a television show. She said words that ring in my ears: "Before I came to America, I didn't know I was poor. I didn't know I was fat. Now I know." Like many refugees, she listens to the music of a foreign country. She gets confused about who she is. Her experience is very similar to that of interfaith families. Before we left our home of origin, everything fit together. Now the famous center does not hold. We can no longer worship one God but must mix our messages. We must decide ourselves whether we are beautiful or ugly, rich or poor. There is a lot of static in our system. Some of it brings truth; some of it simply brings anxiety.

If people in interfaith families believe anything at all in common, it is this slippery, paradoxical nature of truth. Instead of arguing the way the old Christians did — that only by Christ can humanity be saved — we argue that we do not yet know the way to salvation. Maybe we're right; maybe we're wrong. Living without answers is our answer to the question of truth. We think we are "right" in not knowing what is right.

The musical group Sweet Honey in the Rock encourages us to find the truth of our nests and our flights as interfaith people. "We are the people we've been waiting for," they sing. The way they mix up tenses is important for the spiritual refugee. We're not there yet, but we also are. Here is a part of there.

Peter Megargee Brown declares that the true secret of happiness is wanting what we have.[15] What do we have? A religious wilderness. Partnership with the Eagle God — although not the way Moses saw it. Nothing that sounds much like the one, true, universal God we were taught. But nevertheless a God in soaring flight, who is both going away from something and going to something. We just can't see where from our flight deck.

Out here in the deepening and elongating middle, we can be the people we've been waiting for. We could want what we have. We can be happily intermarried, or we can be anxiously intermarried. I prefer the former, mostly because of my Christian fundamentalist background. I was taught the virtue of certainty at an early enough age that risk is now possible. (If I could teach that same certainty to my children — without its accompanying fundamentalism — believe me, I would. I cannot.)

Interfaith families can want what we have. We should not want what others cannot have, in the words of Mahatma Gandhi. We should not want our God to beat their God out. Or to win the religious sweepstakes. We should want a God who looks different from how God is supposed to look.

Interfaith families are nests within nests. We are strangely twigged. Our God has become bird-like, not big and significant, but small and significant. Our God is both an eagle-like bird and a very small bird: we imagine that there are other birds also in sight, not just ours or Moses'. Are we pantheists? Yes. Are we monotheists? Yes — if by monotheism we mean the Bird beyond all the other birds. The God beyond God. Are we confused about who God really is? You bet.

We are emptying ourselves of old certainties on behalf of future capability. We hold memorial services for old hymnals and old tribal gods. We don't know that we are doing these things so much as we just do them. The Eagle God soars above our nest. Also, a little particular bird leads us. Sometimes I am still a strongly affiliated Christian; I do hospice work in the United Church of Christ, my deeply loved employer of twenty-five years. I trust this church and its Christ to understand my confusion as well as my Exodus.

Often members of interfaith families don't even know what we have shaken loose until we see the fragments all over the floor. How do I bury my Jewish husband, if, God forbid, he dies tomorrow? I don't know yet. The Eagle God is flying high, almost out of sight. And the baby bird part of me keeps thinking about trying to jump back into that little world I jumped out of when I married him. My friend speaks of these moments as "Grandma's string of pearls busted, spilling all over the floor."

How do birds fly? By using just the right amount of energy and then by counting on the air. The coefficient of lift is a matter of some consequence to frequent flyers. Ray Bradbury said, "First you jump. Then you get your wings." Members of interfaith families have jumped; we even have a few wings. Like Moses, we aren't sure how long we can carry on with an unknown destination. Must we always float and circle? Probably, for our generation, yes.

If one-third of people now marry outside their faith of origin, there is every reason to believe that percentage will increase over time, through immigration and the resulting propinquity of cultures. For now, in a time of transition between a culture where people married their own kind to a culture where people will often not marry their own kind, we interfaith pioneers believe with Moses that the eagle-like God has stirred her nest. We are less sure of what our tribal God will do and more sure that God will be God. Moses thought that God as eagle stirred the nest tribally. Moses was wrong. God was not there only for the people of Moses. God was also there for the Chinese, the Australians, the Native Americans, none of whom ever heard the name of Israel's tribal God. They heard another Name.

The issue is God. The issue for interfaith families is God. And God is the issue nested within the issue of peace and justice and racism and sexism. God is not small. God is not private. God is not owned by Moses or Confucius or the pope. For God to be God, God must be more than any name. God might even be both large, transcendent and flying and small, incarnate, and close by.

We are in a period in history when these truths about God, this revelation of the God beyond God, is coming to many people. Our frequent flier miles and global Internet access tell us some of the Revelation. The rest is coming from interfaith families, who wrestle with the Eagle God and see her stirring her nest. (Throughout this book, in keeping with the theology being discussed, God will be addressed as "he" or "she" alternately, suggesting the God beyond the captivity of gender in whom the author firmly lives and moves and has her being.)

We interfaith people have a wild mix of tenses within us. We are stranded somewhere between our origins and our destinations. And sometimes, some parts of us even like where we are.

As much as we live in a period of profound revelation of new names for God, the old ones still matter. Where we come from is important. As a child born into a Missouri Synod Lutheran family, I could not have imagined that I would marry a Jew. Or be raising three children both ways.

Or be an ordained (woman!) minister in the United Church of Christ. I am, like many people, a spiritual traveler.

The man I fell in love with at age thirty-four presented me with more than just questions about the many names of God. He gave me name problems of my own. I met Warren Goldstein at Yale while working as a chaplain. He was teaching American Studies and working with a group of students that happened to meet in my office — and the rest is history. We now have three children, Isaac, Katie, and Jacob Goldstein — none with my maiden name, Osterhoudt, or the name of my first husband, Schaper. Yes, this compromise bothers me.

I thought about taking Goldstein because it was most consistent with my previous compromises but decided not to because of the obvious problem of being referred to as the Reverend Donna Goldstein. So here I am. A person with no real name. Or a lot of names. I could go by "Stoner," that compromise suggested by the great feminist Lucy Stone in the nineteenth century. She was purer than I and thought that women should have something of their own to go by. The "Lucy Stoners" thrived for a while, and I suppose if I got desperate, I would join them. "Donna Stoner" has a nice ring. But it would require a new person to go with it — and the main thing I know about myself is that the person I am is all these names and connections, not any one of them. I have origins. I come from a place. I come from one simple nest. I also come from many places. I never even met Lucy Stoner! I have lived with Donna Schaper for a long time.

Problems like these with my name were not imaginable when I was born. Their equal will be imaginable to my children. To my children, pluralism of all kinds is as "normal" as a well-protected German parochialism was in the 1950s. The chance that they could ever worship the God with whom I grew up is practically nil. Their world is too large; its size is at their front door or available with a stroke on a computer keyboard. I did not meet a Moslem until I was thirty: now my children live next door to Moslems.

One of our neighbors is a Jewish and Moslem couple; the other is Moslem and Moslem. All four, like my children's parents, are firm followers of the God beyond God. We also borrow each other's lawn mowers.

Origins matter. Our first nest matters. So do destinations. Our final nesting place, and resting place, matter. We postmoderns live in a world that has changed radically. It is not so small. Toto and many others are not in Kansas any more. And if we are, we are linked by eight hundred numbers, computers, airplanes, and watches in boutique stores that tell us not one time but the time in two locations at once. Unless, of course, they are digitized, and only our children knew how to work them. As theologian Kosuke Koyama puts it eloquently, God does not speak only one language.

Postmodern pluralism and fluidity require a kind of maturity about both origins and destinations. One is open; the other is not. One gives us our identities; the other gives us our challenges. Both matter. I am not a "general" but a "particular." So are you. The more plural things become, the more threatened my potato is in the stew.

One of the measures of maturity is to come to terms with our origins. Birds fly out of real nests. Chickens fly real coops. Maturity connects now to then. It forgives what it needs to forgive and it carries on. Mature people carry their past within them: they don't put it aside. Mature people come from a particular nest; then they fly. God is the origin of the tension of nest and flight. To see this God, we must be willing to peek out of our little nests and check out a few others.

The particularity of our nest matters. It is impossible to

be born as general person. We are born as particular person. Origins matter. Ask your psychiatrist. Or your mother. At middle age, I see how much they matter. My spine is curving the way my mother's curved. My shoulders are as narrow as my father's. I used to think each of these body bends was unattractive. I am learning to love them. I even love the Immanuel Lutheran Church in Kingston, New York. Pastor Witte and my grandmother are both dead now, but they still feather my nest.

Middle age is asking me for a long string of reappraisals: religious reappraisal leads the pack. For the longest time, I loved Jesus Christ as though he were the only face of God. He is not. That knowledge does not diminish Jesus so much as open me. I really don't know how my Jewish husband lives without Christ at the center of history, but I observe that he does. I don't have to understand him to understand that he has a different kind of God than I do. And to know that his God is as ultimate to him as mine is to me. As much as I had hoped to book the grand tour of American exceptionalism and be on the top of every kind of heap, it appears that I will not. I will *not* be different or better than everybody (or anybody) else. The exceptionalism has become too expensive — and gives me a chill.

My unwillingness to pay the price of being "on top," or best, has resulted in an enneagramatic spiritual search. The enneagram is a spiritual tool, developed by the Sufis, that resembles many other spiritual tools. One of its strong arguments is that every asset has a defect. I call my search enneagramatic because it forced me to face diversity between people and the inner diversity of people.[16]

Marrying a Jew has meant I had to look for the assets in my deficiencies, the gifts in my curses. My limitations have their own expansiveness, and I am just getting to know them by name. I have had to make myself the right size. "Had to" is the right way to talk about the verbs of middle tether: we choose what chooses us. All these mixed tenses of becoming the people we are, of wanting what we have and not wanting what others cannot have, of participating in the results of the action, of emptying to fill, all these are appropriate spiritual verbs for interfaith people. We blend as a way of life. We mix tenses as a way of life. We do so on purpose. It is our way of leaning out of the nest, toward flight. We are where we are because we can no longer be where we were.

My origin programmed exceptionalism. But when I left my nest, I looked around. There wasn't that much better about me — and the exceptionalism actually made me worse.

The first breath of maturity outside the nest was flying away from the old small gods. It was no accident that Warren and I fell in love: what we had in common was a fairly clear disgust at the way things were going religiously. We found at the time of our engagement that both Judaism and Christianity were way too small. We loved them and we knew we came from them — and we knew the gifts they had brought. But they fit too tight. They bound. They were as different as blue jeans are to girdles. One fits and is comfortable; the other fits and is uncomfortable.

In our search for something bigger and more comfortable, ironically, we found something much smaller and still more comfortable. This paradox of big and small is central to the experience of interfaith families. Next to the ways origins do matter, the question of size is most significant. We get bigger only to get smaller. We bet on Bethlehem as well as Jerusalem. We get closer to the rootedness of our particular religion while abandoning its universality. We say that we are one of nine types on the enneagram scale and we aren't ashamed to be only one of many.

Kim Chernin says that she too believed earlier in "politics of total commitment on a grand scale" only to change to a point of view that affirmed personal efforts on a small scale.[17] Thoreau spoke of similar downsizing when he acknowledged the youthful hope for a castle transformed to the adult longing for a nice woodshed.

Interfaith families right-size our blend: we don't universalize it. We treasure our origins at the very time that we move beyond them. Because I think so highly of the wealth of interfaith living, do I therefore think it is for everyone? No! It is as valid, though, as Lutheranism is for Lutherans and Judaism is for Jews. It is not bigger, just different. I do hope and pray for the day when "blend" will be as much an option in religious forms as Protestant, Catholic, Jew, Moslem, Buddhist, Hindu, or nothing. I also think that day is coming sooner than the people who write the forms might think.

I have begun to think of my faith as a roomy woodshed, not a mansion or even that embarrassing Protestant "city on a hill." I think of Warren's faith that way too — although Jews have less reason than Christians to think small. Jews stand to lose more than Christians in interfaith living. The reason is proportionality: they are smaller. As Rabbi Stephen Fuchs of Temple Emmanuel in Hartford, Connecticut, put his opposition to interfaith living, the issue is proportion. The partnership, for him, is always unequal.

Respectfully, I think Rabbi Fuchs is wrong: he applies a mathematical power equation in a theological situation, and the equation is inappropriate. More does not mean better — even though many of the power arrangements in our society so indicate. Religion undercuts these power arrangements with Yahweh and with Christ and with Buddha and with the many particular revelations. God always comes with a transforming power: "You," say the genuine Gods, "have heard it said that things are like this…but I say to you that things are another way." Smaller is not inevitably whipped by larger, once God enters the picture.

Instead, interfaith living gives us a glimpse of the nests within nests, twigs laid crosswise upon twigs, the ones that deep down make us capable of flying. The Lutheran theologian Krister Stendahl argues that ancient peoples thought of each of their spots as "the navel of the universe," as a place from which all of God that could be seen was seen. This is what I mean by the little nest inside the big nest: it is a place in both time and space and it is all that there really is, about God or anything else.

One time in Milwaukee I went out looking for a certain spice shop. I wandered for hours and never found it. I had to return to my meeting. On the way back, a certain alley beckoned me to take a shortcut. I almost didn't use the alley for fear. I have not enjoyed being mugged the four or five times I have been so intruded upon. But the alley called my name. It began to smell. Not of ugly garbage but aromatically. Sure enough, on the corner, after I had given up finding it, was the spice shop. These nooks and crannies, turns after turns, accidents within plans, these are the "little" things that make us the kind of spiritual being we are. In nested and blended families, twigs of different origins pile on each other. That's all. Not much more really. Interfaith families have a real headstart on humility. We don't claim capital *T truth*.

Our propinquity in diversity makes it increasingly inevitable that we will fall in love with a twig that came from another part of the world. In a way, my marrying Warren was like finding the spice shop: it just happened. It was like drawing a winning card in a card game and then having to play out the set. I wasn't looking for him, nor he for me, but we did find each other. Isaac, Katie, and Jacob could have come from no other place than this one. We have blended our origins into theirs. That's all. Their nest is tribally richer than either of ours: it is concentrated. And from it they will have to fly.

Chapter Two

Rites and Rights

The moments of most tension for interfaith families are the ritual moments. We try to do them "right" but can't. Thus we double up, compromise, trade, borrow, and create from whole cloth what is tattered and ancient. We do rites instead of right. Baptisms, Brit, marriages, Confirmation, or Bar/Bat Mitzvahs (which my friend irreverently calls "Barmations" or "Mitzvirmations"), burials, any of these normal moments in life become occasions for tension among us.

Our twins had a Baptism service in a Christian church on the South Side of Chicago. A week later we held an informal "home-grown" Brit at our home on the North Side. The first was liturgical in a "regular" Christian way — except that I had asked my dear friend who baptized them to use the words "Creator, Christ, and Holy Ghost" instead of "Father, Son, and Holy Ghost" for the actual baptismal formula. He forgot and used "Father" instead of "Creator." I don't think it made a huge difference — although at the time I could gladly have murdered him. The rite was right enough as it was. At the Brit were a few friends and a lot of Hebrew.

Ritual is the heart of religion. No matter how many courses in cultural anthropology we have taken, many of us still think rites are eternal, that our rites are the right way to do things, despite the fact that there are millions of ways. Tension comes when the presumed eternal collides with the actual bondage to time and place of a ritual. "The way we have always done things" is as close to eternal as most members of most faiths can actually get.

Our family is no different. We develop rites and rituals as we go along: we don't think they are right so much as rite. Our family made a decision to raise our children both Jewish and Christian, not because we knew what we were doing, but, again, because we couldn't think of any other way. We are where we are because we couldn't be where we were any more. I could not convert to Judaism. Warren could not convert to Christianity. A compromise was inevitable. (I have a church that keeps the American flag in the sanctuary half the year and takes it down the other half for the same kind of reason.)

Neither of us is exactly Tevya in *Fiddler on the Roof:* we are not traditionalists. But neither are we anarchists. We forged a compromise about children before we married. We also tried not to marry. We assumed my churches would not approve of my spouse. Instead my Maker gave me five work settings in a row that not only "approved" my marriage but enjoyed it. When we married, I didn't think they existed. I am not sure everyone would be so lucky as to live in institutions friendly to pluralism. This friendliness and Warren's family's openness gave us a base-level permission to experiment with right and rite.

Our compromise included a mutual promise that the children would attend church and Sunday School while they were young and that at Bar and Bat Mitzvah age they would be immersed in Jewish preparation. Thus, the first ten years of their lives occurred in a very Christian context, in which I was also pastor of the church we attended, and the last five years have been in a very Jewish context.

Our parents didn't believe we would follow through on these commitments. When Warren and I married, Warren's mother took to her bed for three days. She saw just exactly how serious this relationship was. From then on, everything important was threatened at its social heart. Her grandchildren might be left without a Bar Mitzvah. She might have to go to services for her friends' grandchildren but not be able to attend those of her own. Eventually, she articulated that her worst fear had been that we would be "throwing the name of Jesus around" at the wedding. As it has turned out, none of these rites of passage have horrified her (yet), but that doesn't mean that her fear was not on target.

Instead of "throwing the name of Jesus around," we put together a wedding service that combined Judaism and Christianity in what we thought was a tasteful way. We purposely did not throw the name of Jesus around — because my faith tells me that Jesus didn't do that himself. So why would we?

We had a very difficult time finding a rabbi who would officiate. Christians were plentiful. Because of our cultural dominance, Christians have much less to lose. We may graciously "include" because we know so little about exclusion. Jews can't include Christians the way Christians can include Jews. This imbalance of power meant that the service had to walk a tightrope. It had to name the God in whom our holy vows were made, but it had to keep the name of that God above all names.

I disagree theologically with rabbis who argue that this inequality means that people should not enter interfaith marriages. I believe that we can but that we must also recognize the depth of the inequality. It is very real, but it does not prohibit intermarriage; rather than making intermarriage impossible, it makes it difficult.

Our naivete in this period continues to amaze me. I should have known, but I didn't. Finally, we found our way to a "marrying Sam," who assured us that he could do the service for $500 — plus gas and tolls. We were appalled, although Warren's family was willing to go ahead with the ceremony. But we dug deeper into Jewish wedding liturgy and discovered an important fact. Jews do not need an ordained professional to be present when the blessings are pronounced. Any Jew can stand for the community in wedding services. Thus it was that a good friend stood with a Christian minister and together they provided "administration," or overseeing, of the service. The universal language of Mozart prevailed, and we managed to stay close to at least one moral principle, which is to do no harm.

In Numbers 15:38–39 we are advised to "put a blue cord on the fringe at each corner.... You have the fringe so that, when you see it, you will remember." Unfortunately, we interfaith people often have to "unfringe" ourselves to get along. We have to be general when particular is much more beautiful.

Interfaith people are less "syncretists" and more "additives," as sociologist Catherine Albanese puts it.[18] We add or double rather than simply mixing. We act like all names for God are good. "Religious mixing is surely the name of the spiritual scene in the U.S today."[19]

Albanese argues that the heart of religious language is gift-giving. If the name of Jesus is perceived not as a gift, but as an insult, why would I use it in a religious service? According to Albanese, "Even spirits go to market, and even spirits, whatever their constraints, purchase gifts." We do purchase and give gifts, most especially at the heart of religious ritual.

Here, what we keep and what we omit is crucial to the gift-giving itself. Compromise in rites is a form of purchase: we are purchasing mutuality and respect of each other.

It is important to observe just how "ritualistic" rituals are in interfaith situations. When we prepared our marriage service, we literally counted who got how many lines. We wanted to even out the theological nods. I have never been surprised that affirmative action is so often a question of numbers. Justice comes from balance. Justice is a destination of interfaith rituals.

Once I was conducting an Arab-Italian wedding at my church in New York. We had a few Moslem prayers, a few Catholic prayers, and me as a liturgical midpoint. There were three flower girls in velvet. The father of the Italian Catholic bride was more than a little inebriated when he got to the service. When he was able to intuit that we were almost done with the service, he stood up and demanded, "Where the hell is the Ave Maria?" At this point, my organist, whom most days I did not fully appreciate, went right into that great hymn with thundering voice and organ. Everyone cried. We had the emotional meltdown we had come for. People relaxed in the middle of the great anxiety that is wedding in America. The music got us beyond the proportionality of dividing prayers up equally. Our wedding, on the other hand, achieved the same transcendence, but only because we carefully divided up the traditions.

I have officiated at the weddings of hundreds of people. I stand behind the altar while people make holy commitments in front of it. I feed them their lines. Some of these commitments last. Many do not, which fact has forced me into sizable dismay about the sacrament of Christian marriage. I have long wondered if the "right rites" were right at all.

Additionally, one of the questions that gay and lesbian

holy unions are forcing is about marriage itself. Many wonder if they want to marry or partner or do something yet invented. As a member of an interfaith tribe, I also wonder. Is there something new we are supposed to be doing that we are not, so intent are we on being accepted by both tribes? Instead of doubling and adding — the higher math of interfaith wedding etiquette — should we experiment with a newly right rite? This question will surface again and again in the generations to come.

For example, are the lines about "better and worse, richer and poorer, till death do us part" a hypocrisy in a disposable culture? Or are they what Toni Morrison calls a "spectacle," which, in contrast to a ritual, is a dramatization of potential truth? Are we playing at commitment in the drama of a wedding?

Marriage has been under assault from more points of view than simply the interfaith one. Charlotte Perkins Gilman, a turn-of-the-century feminist, thought marriage, at its worst, high-class prostitution or, at its best, an inexpensive insurance policy. As women gain economic independence, doesn't one of the strongest supports for marriage disappear?

Margaret Mead argued for a two-tier marriage in our modern Western societies. We should first have a trial marriage with no children and then commit to building the nest that children need to survive. Both religious and economic reasons argue for constant revision of the marriage rite. I am not (yet) advocating divorce or less committed vows: instead, I am wondering what happens creatively to our thought processes once we see that many different kinds of rites can be right. For now we pioneers can expect to be brilliant compromisers and crafty conservatives, but a next generation of interfaith families may take family rituals to new places.

Rituals exist to move people from one place to another.

They are all matters of transition. Baptism and Bar Mitzvah, Brit and Confirmation, marriage, funerals — each is a ritual that takes a person from one developmental stage to another. As a person of faith, I believe in God deeply. I have a sense that God is with me now, later, before, after. Most particularly, God is the thread through transition; rituals thread change for people like me. I don't even think about going on a long trip or leaving a hotel room without some form of prayer or ritual, and likewise I can't imagine major events without ritual observance as well. The problem for interfaith families is that we are in a liturgical and ritual lag. What might have worked to move us developmentally no longer does. And we are slightly embarrassed at having to invent our own liturgies.

Rituals embody spirituality and faith; they bring God near. Janet Hagberg, a feminist theologian, defines spirituality this way:

> Spirituality is an intimate connection with a power beyond us which seeks to dwell within us. Spirituality involves the way we live out our response to that power, the Holy, who invites us to take a courageous inner journey to a place where we have never been before.[20]

She gets close here to a useful framework. It's really not a place we've never been before: we began in a connection with the Holy. We return to it. We are creatures first, creators second. We don't make ourselves. A good ritual touches our original experience of God and continues it. Rituals and rites "practice" spirituality; they rehearse eternity and wholeness for us.

One of the real tightropes that interfaith people walk is in this matter of eternity. Once we have relativized rites, we fear we have also relativized eternity. We have not. But our

rites have lost the certainty of a former power. They float
and fly with us. Rites are fluid but we imagine them solid.
Rites change over time, in response to changes in cultures,
economies, and people. They cohere by changing.

Some interfaith people will want to choose one ancient set
of rites so that they do not have to confront this constant
shifting of the sense of the sturdy. Conversion is a very appealing option precisely because it indulges one historically
valid set of patterns rather than juggling and mixing several.

Judy Petsonk and Jim Remsen say that about a third of
intermarrieds choose to observe the faith of both partners.[21]
Others convert to one of the faiths; still others abandon
faith. In this pioneer period, clearly there are a hundred flow-
ers blooming. Our blend is our way, no more, no less. We
tried to achieve parity when we got married; we ignored that
criterion for the Baptism and Brit of the twins. Isaac, the
oldest, was only baptized. Consistency is not our strong suit.

What we wanted to avoid in our compromise was sec-
ularism or "Sheilaism," the completely noncommunal and
antihistorical selfishness described by Robert Bellah and colleagues in *Habits of the Heart*.[22] Asked to name her faith, a
woman named Sheila coins the absurdity "Sheilaism." This
very popular book argues that the American compromise
elevates a private God for individual use while the public
realm is on its own morally. Both Warren and I abhor this
compromise. We were subversives early on.[23]

In addition to ordinary interfaith dilemmas, we have enjoyed those that result from subversion. Our compromises
were not just between us and our traditions of origin but
also between us and cultural or civil religion. Our concern at
the beginning was not so much about our or the children's
preparation for eternity as it was about who they would be
in this life. We wanted them to be good public people as

well as good private people, good people in the board room and marketplace as well as good at home. By whom would they be stranded? We did not want to throw them into a completely individualized world, orphaned from both their religious traditions and their culture. Any American child can be a "Sheila" without the slightest embarrassment. Frank Sinatra comes to mind, singing his popular song, "I Did It My Way."

Leslie Goodman-Malamuth and Robin Margolis show how children's sense of the eternal and the sturdy has been assaulted fairly early in their lives.[24] Many children also experience a not very pretty competition between their parents for adherence. In our family, the question of which of our faiths will claim our children is sometimes a subversion of a subversion. We agree on a public faith; we also agree that both our faiths of origin are *not* Sheilaistic. Our conflict is peculiar: we agree more than we disagree. We agree to subvert. But the children still live in a culture where Sheila reigns.

Rites and rights impact matters of eternity, matters of intimacy, matters of spectacle, and matters of truth. They also involve every interesting and complex family interaction. No wonder the night before a big event very few of us sleep! No wonder we worry about the "food"! The more important issues are too hard for most of us to manage.

In addition to the competitions and the subversions and the normal complexities of doing a rite right, interfaith families have particularly interesting extended family issues. Among the social participant-observers the grandparents are extremely important to what makes a rite or ritual effective in connecting children to God. In *Mingled Roots: A Guide for Jewish Grandparents of Interfaith Grandchildren,* Sunie Levin offers grandparents dozens of ways to bless and not curse.[25]

As our hybrid seeds begin to grow, we learn more about what our nests within nests are. There are strong fears of separation from our roots, there are ridiculous competitions (like which gets the bigger gift budget, Christmas or Hanukkah), and there is simple ignorance of each other's patterns. Interfaith families need to combine all their rites and rituals with a lot more conversation than others. This conversation can be tedious, but it can also be wonderful.

Because rites and rituals make ordinary time into sacred time, we are often blessed with a feeling of great unity during them, only to find that unity fragmented over a small thing like saying a Jewish word wrong. Our "sacred canopy" (as Peter Berger called the religious world) is a little tattered from time to time, but it lets a lot of holy air through. We are not able to brag about our experiment so much as to tell its truth, and sometimes its truth is hard.

The little rituals often tell more than the big ones, like marriage and children's rites of passage. We celebrate a very simple Sabbath on Friday nights, with two prayers, a few candles, and a blessing for the children. Our nightly prayer is one with hands, not with words at all, which is a superb compromise in my own view. The children's good night prayers are more conversation than prayer.

Interfaith for us means that we like the separation as much as the combination. People send our interfaith family a lot of sensitive "happy holidays" cards — but we'd prefer the Hanukkah lights on their day and the Christmas Christ on December 25 — "straight up." As an interfaith family we believe in stew, not melting pot. Others want something different — and that is their choice.

In our family, the menorah does get placed very close to the Christmas tree. We even have uncomfortable pictures of both together. The reason is less theological than practical. The one season blends into the other, and both symbols have meaning for us. Little children cavort in front of them, and we snap photos. While it is important to reflect on why and how these December connections happen, it is more important to let them be gifts from God. "Lighten up" is an important message for those of us who think too much about getting rites right.

Sometimes we blend. And sometimes we don't. The menorah and the tree may both be in our living room simultaneously, but that doesn't mean we are combining them. Hanukkah does not compare well to Christmas: one is a minor festival in the Jewish faith and the other a major Christian festival, and it is unfortunate that they are compared as equals, particularly since the meaning of the Hanukkah observance is anti-Hellenization or anti-mixing. It is as if a minor Christian festival like All Saints' Day was paired with Rosh Hashanah and Yom Kippur.

How can we affirm both and affirm them at different times in different ways? Isn't religious truth so eternal and monotheistic that only one God and one faith dare be observed? I think not. Neither does God speak only in Jewish or only in Christian terms. God also speaks in Moslem terms. The sooner we get beyond simplistic "right-answer" gods to humbly accessing the God beyond God, the better.

In this time of institutional religious lag, there are at least a thousand right ways of being faithful as an interfaith family. Those who keep the tree and the menorah separate and distinct have their argument about purity of tradition, and it is a good one. Those who blend into the middle find God there as well. Or, better put, they find the God beyond God, which is the one we are trying to worship in our both/and approach.

The story of the last Easter/Passover coincidence is illustrative. I approach these seasons with Duncan Maclean, the Irish poet, who wants God to throw a brick through his window. I want a religious experience. What I usually get is more frequent flyer miles. We sometimes go to Washington for Passover and Good Friday to be with Warren's family, especially now that I work regionally rather than parochially. The flight usually sets us back over a thousand dollars.

On our most recent expedition Jacob, my humorist, had carried a jar of gherkins and a box of toothpicks onto the plane. He passed them out for a "little snack." That kind of goofballing often helps assuage religious as well as physical hunger.

Then during a stop at Kennedy Airport a terrible rainstorm prevented our continuing on the next leg of our trip and kept us in Jamaica, Queens, overnight — at our expense because the delay was weather related. Maundy Thursday found us in a small hotel room with the five of us watching *As Good As It Gets,* in which Jack Nicholson proves that the most unlovable are quite lovable and can find each other. I found this deeply right to solace my religious urgency. The only food we had in the hotel was the apples for the Hirosis and the boiled eggs I had brought for the Easter basket. We spent fifteen dollars for a toothbrush (only in New York) and shared it after the eggs and apples. Some Last Supper memorial!

The next morning we were, of course, starving. I went down to the breakfast buffet at about 6 a.m. It was a bounty — but cost $16.95. I ordered one meal and began to stuff my pockets with bread and Danish for the rest of the family. Down came Jacob, bereft of pickles. "I give you two for the price of one," announced the waiter in his Middle Eastern accent. Embarrassed, I agreed to his generosity. Down came Katie. "No problem. I give you three for the price of one." I considered putting some of the Danish back. Down came Isaac. "No problem. I give you four for the price of one." I turned purple: it was dawn of Good Friday and here I was receiving the generosity of one from whom I had stolen bread. I told Duncan Maclean he could stop now. Down came Warren. The waiter said, "Problem."

We left soon, very soon, and continued our trip to Washington. I spent three hours at the National Cathedral worshiping my heart out and beginning to glimpse what this suffering God is all about. A Gregorian chant nearly broke my heart. Yes, I was late for the family Passover dinner, but I thought it started at sundown. My husband angrily assured me it started with cocktails.

The next day, Easter Saturday, my in-laws took the kids to the Holocaust museum and the kids were intensely interested. I was thrilled. Jacob has been quoting the famous words of Martin Niemoller — When they came for the Gypsies, etc. — and I can't believe how much he understands about that. More bricks are crashing through more windows.

I put chocolate dreidles in the interfaith Easter basket; the kids went by themselves to a Presbyterian Easter service on Sunday morning. Warren and I snuck off to worship in Martinsburg, West Virginia, where I graduated from high school.

When we got back to Kennedy on Sunday night, we found out that our continuing flight had been cancelled. After a long bus ride, just as midnight closed out Easter for the year, Katie went to work on her uncompleted science project. Not all of our rites are this right. But some are. God gets through even closed windows.

Chapter Three

Whence Fundamentalism?

The real enemy of our nests within nests is fundamentalism. The trouble is not with fundamentals but with the way they are distorted and become an "ism." If something is important to us, it does not have to be absolute. Religious fundamentals begin as revelations of truth and goodness — and then they are reduced to absolutes with a regularity that is quite frightening.

I think of my favorite story about our new UCC Hymnal, called the *New Century Hymnal*. It is replacing a book we called the *Pilgrim Hymnal,* which was completed in 1953. Before that there was another book, and before that another one. Hymnals, like scriptures, are not once-and-for-all things but for-this-time events. Nevertheless, a parishioner once said to me in the midst of the fight in his parish over replacing *Pilgrim* with *New Century* that "if the *Pilgrim Hymnal* was good enough for the Pilgrims, it is good enough for me." He assumed that since he had known only this one hymnal, then it must have existed forever. He canonized his culture.

Canonized fundamentalism makes interfaith families feel like discounted religious goods. Fundamentalists put us down for living with fresh religious revelation instead of stale. Jews are said not to be Jews if they go with the Goyim. Christian credentials are similarly (although not as vitriolically) suspect. Ironically a true Jew or a true Christian is hardly a fundamentalist at all but rather one for whom history and experience have been opened by God.

Today we see the fundamentalist battle most clearly in the coded language of "family values." Neither Jesus nor Torah laid anything down about these matters, but people like to think they did. They hope for a once-and-for-all *Pilgrim Hymnal,* and what they find when they go to Holy Writ is an opening to new music and to genuine family, not "family values."

What do interfaith families value? Are we different in what we value? Or do we just value our difference? Does our difference refine or get in the way of our knowing God? Does "interfaith" get in the way of faith or does it enrich faith? I believe that it does more of the latter but I know it does both.

When it comes to "family values," we interfaith people need to know our social location, what the Germans call our *Sitz im Leben,* our site in life. We need to know if there is anything different about our family values as compared to those of Catholics or Jews or Protestants or Sufis.

I fear that there is not. But that lack of difference is less about interfaith choices than it is about the power of culture to determine values. This power is the first layer of understanding of who God is for any of us, no matter our location. Cultures use fundamentalism to support themselves; it is culture that turns fresh religion into stale bread.

In our culture, we live with the religion of "Sheila." Interviewed by Bellah and colleagues, Sheila said she didn't quite have a distinct faith. Rather she believed in God, generally, and in herself, to the point of saying, "You could call my faith Sheila-ism."

Most of us are right in there with her. What matters more to us than our faith of origin is the profound permission given to individualism and individual expression by our culture. A Protestant, a Catholic, a Jew, or a member of an interfaith family is as likely to be "Sheila-istic" as not. We are self-promoters, and we believe we are supposed to be self-supporters. The values of increase, growth, "making money," and the individual's responsibility to do so rival any religious value of any American religion. To be sure, there are pockets of lively exception. I think of the Amish, some of the Quakers, certain fundamentalist groups, and immigrant faiths. But, on the whole, in my interfaith family and in most of those I know, the values of American culture are our family values. Our religious faith is routinely hauled out to legitimate the values of individualism and its social companion, capitalism, but in fact our faiths of origin have little blessing for what we practice, with Sheila, as family values.

We live in a tension between religion and culture. Interfaith families experience as much tension between our faith and our culture's values as do strict Jews or Christians. Deep inside so-called American family values there are golden rules and religious fidelities. But rare is the family value that is perceived as godly or transcendent or vertical: these values are humanistic, immanent, and horizontal. They are ways we are supposed to behave toward each other rather than toward God.

This point about humanism and its distinction from religious faith is crucial to any family that is thinking about what matters. To get to the bottom of our nest we need to travel through all the twigs, all the way down.

The golden rule is the bedrock American "rule," but it is

quite fully misinterpreted. In the scriptural golden rule, we are to love God first with all our heart and soul and mind — and then love our neighbor as ourselves. Jesus was quoting the commandments of the Hebrews. Judaism and Christianity have this rule in common. And both humanize it. The rule forgets God. It buries God deep within the nest. What happens on the surface is what matters. We matter. Sheila matters. Even our neighbor matters. But the source of matter doesn't matter. God is eclipsed.

Thus, when it comes to family values, interfaith families often have a lot in common with single-faith families. Compounding the problem of culture's victory over particular religion, humanism has had a victory over all religion. God is as much a problem for those with two faiths as those with one faith. Routinely, when we use consultants to help with conflict in our UCC parishes, the consultant concludes that a kind of "functional atheism" prevails, that is, the near complete forgetting that God has something to do with church or might be available to help us with our quarrels with one another. God does not get mentioned — even in the middle of life-threatening battles within parishes. People have to dig deep to "remember" God, so dominant is humanism in our culture.

Within this culture, with my origin in Christian faith and my adopted Jewish commitments, inside this nest and its various nooks and crannies, I have three children to raise. I hear about family values everywhere, but what I hear has nothing to do with the Christianity I practice or the Judaism my husband observes. Both of these faiths are graceful at their heart; they embody forgiveness. They know the God of the second chance. They indicate by their very existence that God can yet do something new and more with human history. They are both about God, who is at the bottom of the bottom of the nest. They are about God and not about us. If there is significance to humanity, the significance is godly. We are creatures, not self-created. We are important because we are important to God. We are important because God acts in our personal and our social history.

Our culture tells us, in contrast, in constant sloganeering about family values, that values are rules and that values are humanistic in their source. In this diminishment of family values, there are rules about raising children, which involve obedience to parents, getting ties on straight, making sure to have good posture, making sure not to know about sexuality too early, making sure gays and lesbians are anathema, and the like. In my community, we were nearly not allowed to have a photo exhibit of gay families in the local school because of "family values." Censorship apparently is a family value. What God thinks of individuals who are gay was simply not a matter of discussion. Families use values to control each other into acceptable social behavior.

The conflict between those who permit such exhibits and those who prohibit them has ancient religious roots. On the one hand, there are those who love the law and practice the politics of purity. These are people who live life by recipe and use measuring spoons on their personal morality. Their children's moral growth is stunted by stinginess and self-righteousness.

The other side includes those who see Jesus as the *telos*, or end, of the law. These people live by compassion, not purity. They live in the much less pure and more open system of golden rule love. Their children are often confused about what really to do. They join a long and beautiful line of people in being less than certain that every question has a neat answer. They know God as the source of their value — not anything "obedient" they do or do not do.

In both the purity strain and the more graceful strain of faith, we confront the godlessness of current practice. Both purity and forgiveness abhor functional atheism. Both side, instead, with a powerful, involved God.

This God does pay a visit to the Sheilas of the world from time to time, not to give them permission to "be themselves" so much as to bind them to the self of God. Sheila really believes all of life is up to her. Individualism sneaks into perfectionism so easily that it rarely needs or wants room for the gracious, forgiving, second-chance, in-charge God. The religion of individualism is idolatrously anti-God because it places humans in charge of the life that God owns. It also places one individual in competition and conflict with another: if God is active in history, which both Jews and Christians adamantly believe, then God is active and involved with humanity, with everyone, not just some. Individualism elevates individuals. God elevates the "people" of Israel.

These bindings of God to Israel, which both Christians and Jews understand as fundamental, are the complete law and the complete love of God. In these bindings, the various strains of biblical thought cohere. Jesus repeated the Hebrew rule in Matthew 5, that the first order of righteous living was to love God, first, foremost, and with all that we have. The second is to love our neighbor as we love ourselves. "On this," said Jesus, "hangs all the law and the prophets." Elsewhere, he said that he came to fulfill (*plerosai*) the law and prophets. *Plerosai* means to clarify the true meaning. Jesus clarifies, for some, the true meanings of the sacrificial system and the purity systems.

Love centers the law. As good as the law is, love is even better. Love is not the enemy of law; love is the completion of law. What is important about the value of love is that

God loves us. God wants to be in relationship with us. The rest follows from that loving relationship with God, not our goodness or deserving.

My children and I have played a little game for a long time. The three of them ask who I love the most. I say that on Mondays I love Isaac the most, on Tuesdays I love Katie the most, on Wednesdays I love Jacob the most. And then I change it and make a confusing puzzle of which days belong to which child. By the time I have them giggling, I tell them the real truth: that I love God the most, even more than any one of them. They have come to love/hate this moment in the game. "Here it comes," they'll say. "Watch out. She's going to tell us about God."

What I as a Christian mean when I refer to family values is to love God first and my neighbor second. I cannot idolatrize even my own children. Even they can't be first in my life. Do I sin in this regard? Absolutely. All the time. I sin as a mother because I often put my children before God.

My battle with the civic faith of American culture (and its new frightening codification in the Christian Right) is fierce and humble on this point. I do not believe that women and mothers like me are meant to put our "families first." We are to put God first. Even women are allowed to try to be fully Christian. The golden rule is not for men only. I know that I do idolatrize my children. But I still have the right to try to be a good Christian! That right involves compassion for all my neighbors and not just my own flesh and blood. It means that I love other mothers' children the way I love my own. It means that I am to love a "welfare" mother's children with the fierceness that I love my own.

The Hebrews understood the depth of the sin of idolatry. Even loving "others" more than we love God is idolatry.

Everyone we love is not deserving of our love. The golden

rule does not suggest that we love only those who deserve our love. It is silent on that question, implying rather
eloquently that we are to love the unlovable and the undeserving the way we love ourselves.

Think of the poor, who are to many both unlovable and
undeserving. Poverty in the scheme of the golden rule is simply a problem; it does not deserve shame. Shame is reserved
for idolatry. Jesus didn't see poverty as sinful, and neither
do golden rule Christians. Some of us remember growing up
poor and not feeling ashamed of what we didn't have. We
are intellectually and morally embarrassed by the idolatrous
Christian Right and the way it blames the poor for poverty.
We see the source of this blaming in the purity codes, for-
tified by individualistic "family values" to embarrass both
Christians and Jews. As the stock market grows and people
make more money than they dared imagine, but still more
and more people are left behind by the economic juggernaut,
it becomes harder to comprehend the idolatrous claim that
poor people are bad and that's why they are poor.

The opening verses of Matthew 5 made this value of God
first paramount. Ironic, isn't it, that the so-called Christian
Right is advising flagrant violation of the biblical injunc-
tions? Jesus elsewhere says that any one who would not leave
mother or father or sister or brother for him cannot be his
disciple. When I practice golden rule Christianity and try to
be compassionate toward my neighbor, I am trying to follow
Jesus as best I can. I am not a follower of Jesus who disdains
those who do not follow Jesus, for example, the Jews. Jesus
would not disdain them; nor may I.

The wager of the gospel is fundamentally different from
the wager of the Christian Right. The gospel wagers that
there is plenty of love to go around, that by basing our life
in God first and each other second, we will actually multiply

our capacity for mutual support and caring. The Christian Right assumes that there is so little that we better take care of our own first. Their assumption is wrong — and thus it is no wonder that it spews hatred into the body politic. "Fear not," Jesus said, regarding life properly ordered by God first. Hatred comes from fear that there is not enough. There is.

There might even be enough for me to come to be compassionate toward the totalitarian fear and hatred of the religious Right. For that compassion I pray. It is one of the family values I am trying to teach my children.

How am I doing? In certain ways, terribly. I don't love my children all the time any better than I love God. I am fortunate that my ethical system is not based on purity or perfection.

A popular maxim proclaims that love is leaning on someone to hold that person up. I lean on my children for meaning, for order, for direction. I am not the only person ever to have used children this way. I doubt that assuaging my own fear of my own mortality is my primary purpose in caring for my children, but it is one of the reasons. I also have unselfish regard for my children but I would be lying to say that unselfishness is all.

Being a mother has been harder than anything I have ever had to do. I remember when the children were young and in their big English buggy. People would stop me on the street in Chicago and point to the three under two. "Don't worry: it will get much harder once they are older."

Now I know they were right. The children now have pain that I can't stand. A best friend rejects one in fifth grade. A birthday party invitation, long expected, doesn't arrive. One gets tweaked in the behind by a tall kid in junior high. One remains the shortest kid in the eight grade — and has to go to school, every day, any way. The older they are, the longer it takes them to stop crying. Their pain is my pain.

Being a mother means tending. It means understanding our own neediness as well as our children's and not being afraid of either. Being a mother is nesting work. The nest must be strong at the same time that it is free and free-ing.

These matters, questions of God and idolatry, are much more important to faith than are the questions of blended faiths. They also make most of the current debate about family values seem small and silly. They are common questions, matters we hold in common. They deserve the attention of the person or family who would live within the nest within the nest. When we get off these questions, into the purity questions of whose God is bigger or better, we are simply sophisticating the base idolatry of American cultural religion. When religious questions focus their light and attention on people, they are often ignoring God. Leaning how to focus on God and God's grace for us is *the* religious question. It transcends interfaith questions. And it also grounds them.

I think often of a profound image from the art world, that of the Zodiac Tychee. Both Cincinnati's art museum and the Jordanian government owned a piece of the ancient sculpture. Each claimed the other's piece. Jordan claimed national, original ownership; Cincinnati argued it came by its fragment legally through purchase. Finally the two museums agreed to make a cast of its fragment and share it with the other so a representation of the whole piece could be displayed by both. Each acknowledges that its piece lacks the original perfection. I mother out of recognition of my own incompleteness. As a member of an interfaith family, I think of myself as incomplete and partial. God completes me. I do not complete God.

Elizabeth Barrett Browning said, "All that I had Hoped to

Be and Was not / Comforts Me." I mother from both com-
pleteness and incompleteness. These two are my rules. They
are my "family values." I doubt that either Christianity or
Judaism, or even together, are enough to support my children's future. They will need the God beyond the God of
religion, the God beyond the God of any religion. A few rules
won't hurt them either. Knowing I cannot give my children
all that they will need, I give them what I have.

What I have is imperfect love. What God gives is perfect
love. Mothers place conditions on our love; God does not.
Mothers love like old sow bears. Sue Hubbell reminds us of
this kind of mother love when she tells the story of the kind
of love she felt for her firstborn son the moment he was born.
She called the love "uncivilized, crude, unquestioning, unrea-
soning." She tells us that "in order to become an adequate
mother, I had to learn to keep the old sow bear under control. Sow-bear love is a dark, hairy sort of thing. It wants to
hold and protect; it is all emotion and conservatism. Raising
up a child in the twentieth century to be independent, strong,
capable and free to use his wit requires other kinds of love.
Keeping the sow bear from making a nuisance of herself may
be the hardest thing there is to being a mother."[26]
Social scientists tell us the same thing. They say that the
best mothers are the ones who learn to let go, who live not
through their children but beside them. The better mothers
become God-like, but not perfect. The best mothers forsake
fundamentalism and its perfection.

Child psychologist Carole Klein writes, "Competence as a
mother has to do with how successful one is in viewing one's
children as separate from oneself."[27] She says that the chief
need of children is to be enjoyed, not protected. They need
to see that their mother is happy and then they can be happy.
If all she is doing is protecting them, they become fundamen-

tally afraid of life. If Mom sees that much danger, there must be that much danger. If Mom sees happiness around each corner and under each stone, there must be happiness.

A parent's job is to lead her children to God. She should keep the children safe enough from harm so that they can dedicate their lives to God. She has to be very careful that her children do not dedicate their lives to her. That would be idolatry. She has to provide enough security so that the children can consider higher purposes and higher goals, so that they not spend their lives finding security but rather finding joy and freedom and eventually God.

God does not overprotect us. God could intervene more in our lives but does not. God lives a godly life and sets us free to live a human life. We do not live to please God but rather to praise God. What we know is that God enjoys us. Anoints us. Is in love with us. Is nearby but not meddling. There is a wisdom in the love of God that saves us from anxiety. If God were protecting us every minute like an anxious mother sometimes does, we would begin to get very afraid. What is the danger that requires God's constant intervention? I frequently ask this question of the fundamentalists. Their God meddles frequently in their daily lives — providing a parking space if they need one, or a proper passage if they but turn the page, or healing from a sore throat — for theirs is a world of enormous danger. A world they can't handle themselves. A world in which they depend so fully on God that they can't depend on themselves. I am fearful of this world and this God. And grateful that it is not the God of the scriptures but rather the God of an overactive imagination. The scriptural God is not a sow-bear God: she or he — and we know that God is way beyond either of those words — is a loving God, one who sets us free not to fulfill the ambitions of an underdeveloped God but rather to fulfill ourselves. We do not have to do what God could not do in saving the world. We may save the world, but we are so radically free that we don't have to do that.

Yes, if we are to make our children free, we have to let them fail us. Like God has let humanity fail him. Our children are not our children. They are not our possessions. They do not exist to do what we think ought to be done. God is like a Father or Mother to us. We are not possessed by God. We can choose to do God's will, but we do not have to do God's will in order to command God's love. We get that anyway.

A second way, besides freedom, that a good mother's love is like God's love is in its capacity for other and larger relationships. You would think that God would want us to love only God, that God's love would be jealous and demanding and exclusive. Love me to the exclusion of all others. When God sent Jesus, we got precisely the opposite advice. It is a very interesting choice by God to be loved by us through our love for others. You know the two commandments. The first is to love God, with all our heart, soul and mind. And the second is to love our neighbors as ourselves. They are linked, inseparable. You can't do just one. You can't love your neighbor without loving God. And you can't love God without loving your neighbor. This is how Jesus puts it.

Oedipus, thousands of years ago, whom we now know through the Oedipus complex, exemplified a permanent triangle in the matter of love. Seen from the child's perspective, it is the child's jealousy of the mother's love for the father. Seen from the father's perspective, it is his jealousy for the love the mother gives the child. This triangle is very real. (I've always wanted to know how this triangle looks from the mother's perspective but almost no one is really interested!) Ask any father of a newborn baby. He will tell you all about it. And psychologists will tell you that most marriages fail because the parents don't navigate the heavy-duty waters of having children. They start to live through and for the children rather than for each other. They love the children too much, and the children figure out how to get between the mother and the father.

God's love provides a very interesting contrast to Oedipal love. God says that to love God you must love each other. God refuses to be triangled against humanity. God refuses to play the game of who is loved the most, saying over and over again that each is loved the most. But, we say, you can't love me the most and her the most? And over and over God says, "Oh, yes I can. Not only that but if you want to love me, love each other." God's love gives us a very good model for mother's love. It is a refusal to overprotect. And it is a refusal to triangle, a refusal to make choices of husband over children or children over husband. It is actively being your own person, as a child of God, so that neither husband nor children own you or your love. It is a refusal to play their game, the game called most. And that refusal opens up God's game, the game of love where there is always enough for each and every one, every child, every husband, every mother.

Interfaith families don't live only in family contexts. We live a hypercontextual life. We live between tribes but still within tribes, with double the weddings, rituals, and rites of passage. We have almost too much to value. Families that love God first value the depth of their religious tradition but not its distorted fundamentalism nor its flattening contextualization. We value God first and all the rest second.

We are as enticed by the false security of fundamentalist answers to life's questions as anyone else. But it is an option that our experience denies — and for that we are very grateful.

Chapter Four

Spiritually Rich Children

In the last chapter we talked about how negative fundamentalism can be, especially for interfaith families. When we are coming from a diverse set of sources, we want nothing so much as to have a genuine touch with God. We have reason to fear heresy more than most. Fundamentalist disdain for us is oddly a gift: our being called impure or diluted or bad and wrong forces us to ping the crystal of our faiths.

Even without fundamentalist accusations, we have our own suspicions about ourselves. Just because we did something doesn't necessarily mean it is right. Authenticity is something we love even more than most people!

Spiritually rich families enjoy well-pinged fundamentals and foundations. Spiritually rich families enjoy open foundations, ones that carry the weight of religious truth but carry it lightly. Fundamentalism closes foundations. Interfaith families do best to tell the truth about the transition that we inhabit. That fluid truth becomes the foundation for our children. We open our foundations to future revelation from God.

Families are, for better or worse, authentic places. Not much gets hidden in a family. Families are also the nests where God's touch is nested and taught and expected. Family is the place where phoniness can't really survive. We know each other too well. Thus family is the place we call home, the place where we take off our masks.

Children are the most truthful of all humans. We didn't need Art Linkletter to remind us that kids say the darnedest things. They do because they are always listening for the truth — and because nobody has told them that "there are just some things you can't say." Children seek and speak truth. They also seek and speak home.

Developmentally, we watch children become adults and lose touch with truth: they begin to say what is expected of them rather than what is true. Most adults face a developmental crisis and find ways to become "themselves" again. This second naivete (Paul Ricoeur's wonderful term) is the time when adults join the children in their families to find and know God. Interfaith families thank children for honesty, fundamentalists for challenges, and God for being willing to inhabit a transition as well as a stable place.

We hear, even in transition, the Shema: "Hear, O Israel, the Lord our God is one" (Deut. 6:4). We hear the command to love God with all our hearts, souls, and might and to teach our children to walk in the way of the Lord (in Deut. 6:5–9). We follow these commands in the transition in a transitional way. We try to give our children a spiritual home, even if it is a fluid one.

Mimi Doe says that God is in the details of parenting.[28] Parents worry about the big questions of heresy; children worry about supper. Religious development goes through the stages from trust to generativity just as much as any other kind of development.[29]

In the beginning, children must simply know that God cares for them and that all life is connected and has purpose. There is simply no reason to burden a child with theological conflicts. Instead, we may bless them with religious certainties and trust.

Instead of hearing complaints from adolescents and young adults about religious confusion, I hear complaints about the lack of truth in the religious stories told to them. The complaint I hear most often is against hypocrisy, not against confusion. Roy Blount, Jr., talks about the relationship between him and his mother: "Why did we sing that song about 'red and yellow, black and white, precious in his sight,' if we didn't mean it?"[30] Many adults want to get free of their parents' partial truth, not their confusion.

Still, many people fear that interfaith families confuse children: we say that there are multiple sources for the things that other people say have only one. We complicate their lives early. In my experience, they don't really mind, if truth is the friend of the complication. God remains the one that Israel hears, but people don't all see the same God.

Many people also complain that interfaith families make it "hard" on children. I think differently: I think we make "truth" on children. And truth is hard in its mature and complicated forms, but truth is easy in its simple early forms. Open truth is an honest foundation for children of any developmental stage.

I am not demeaning the fears of those opposed to interfaith living. They have a point about the children and their religious confusion. They have more of a point in worrying about the Oedipal issue: if one parent's faith is chosen over another at some point in life, surely there will be hurt. But interfaith parents have as much a right as anyone else to offer their values to their offspring and, if an interfaith blend is the family's choice, why might it not also be the child's choice? If the adults in the family have made a choice to live on the road, not tribally, but in motion, why might the children not do so also? Trust, connection, and love are part of the road as well as part of the home.

Joan Hawxhurst advises clarity about which services your family will and won't observe.[31] Clarity is very important to children: we communicate clarity to them by making decisions with the authority we have as their parents. Rather than being "lost in the confused sea of postmodernism" as one of my critics put it, attempting "to appropriate a little truth from here and a little truth from there," I believe I am swimming in that sea. Not drowning, but swimming. Sometimes even floating. I find the sea a safe and trusting and connecting place.

I mark off the area where my children are to swim — but I don't act as if the ocean is not there. The reason for the clarity and the bounding of one area is that there are different developmental realities for adults and children. Adults may be able to nest on the road, but children need homes. They are the genuine conservatives among us. They have and need patterns: they like to have everything just right. Change their seats at the table and they complain. Alternate the night on which we "always" have clam chowder and you will know it. Make them feel homeless and they will act out. Symbols are very important to the child's imagination. Whatever religious truth we communicate to youngsters, it is very important that we communicate it clearly and simply and without the anxiety that comes only at later developmental stages. Open truth that is not anxious manages these complexities; anxious truth, whether open or closed, either does not.

All three of my children would like more pattern in their lives. They would always like both parents at home on weekends, and they would always like to have their supper exactly at six o'clock. We have denied them such regularity.

One year's Yom Kippur was emblematic in its irregularity. We just barely managed to clothe the children in new outfits, by means of a mad, irreligious, and unholy dash to the mall right before services. Tags were being ripped off as yarmulkes were being put on. Who would have anticipated they had grown that much over the summer? They also had soccer that day, as well as saxophone lessons. We had to cancel sports practice and music lessons at the last minute, throwing our little digitalized Mussolinis into quite a tizzy. They announced that they hated Yom Kippur and religion; both are too disruptive of their coveted regularity.

We rationalize that we are not preparing the kids for regularity but for irregularity in a regular, homey sort of way. We are preparing them for spiritual adventure, not spiritual comfort. They mightily prefer comfort. Thus, home is one thing for them and another for us. We live in different desires. We differ in our fantasies about what home should be. Home is this tension: it is regularly irregular.

Children can't stand the paradox that adults come to love. They want things to be either this or that, either black or white, either now or precisely at a certain moment later. We are trying to teach them a high nesting pattern that includes, rather than excludes, tension. It is not easy, and that lack of ease is a distinct part of our home-schooling curriculum.

Mary and Martha explain my point better than I can. In the biblical story, Martha does all the housework and Mary does all the "spiritual" work. I can't stand either of them: Martha for letting Mary run her around; Mary for splitting off her body from her soul. Dishpan hands aren't holy; prayer is. Balderdash.

We are trying to teach our children both body and spirit, both dress clothes and Yom Kippur, both comfort and adventure, both regular and irregular, both ease and difficulty.

We are trying to teach our children both family and village. We are trying to teach our children about a God who escaped from fundamentalism's jail. She is larger than any of the tribal faiths imagine. There is every possibility that all these things are "too much " for children, but lying to them would be so much worse that we are condemned to a rich and complex blessing/curse.

If my children want more comfort and order in their lives, they will have to work toward it themselves. I could more perfectly fill my children's needs if they would become more like Martha. All they have to do is help with the housework. Until I get their help with the house, I'll tell be stuck in paradox. I may even get stuck between Mary and Martha.

In our house, Mom is not alone in being in charge of the bodies (laundry, food, dust), and Dad is not alone in being in charge of meditation in the lazyboy. Everybody gets some dust, including kids, and everybody gets some rocking chair. My children join most children in thinking they are overworked and underappreciated. Without their labor, this operation would completely sink. Now it only sinks every couple of days.

One day my oldest son said, "All you want me to do is to clean up my room. That's all you want from me." Then he burst into nine-year-old tears. I know exactly how he felt. Sometimes I fear that my family loves me only because of my services to them, the way I organize and administer and prepare their lunches and lives. The other side of that picture is none too pretty either. I've known kids who were just useless. Nobody needed them at all. They were little decorations on the mantelpiece, mannequins to dress up. Ever since we have had our goats (yes, goats) our children have been needed to feed and water them. It has changed their personality. Without hurting the goats. It has taught them the elusive nature of comfort. The goats have shown that to get comfort, you must be able to give some.

These complexities — religious education through details — prepare the children for the larger and more fundamental complexity of a God who is more the both/and type and less the either/or type. These domestic complexities undermine simplistic thinking and do so intentionally. The message *is* complexity. The more clarity and trust and connection parents give children, the more capable they will become of complexity. Basic trust prepares us for basic complexity.

My own imperfections had taught me that paradox long before either children or goats came along. I learned early how to talk on the phone while cleaning the sink. Children then taught me that you could load the groceries while someone is trying to pull off your wraparound skirt in the parking lot. Paradox allowed me to continue to hum, even under such circumstances. Yom Kippur services will probably always be a bit of a rush. Homes are for going out and for coming in, from this day forward, even for evermore.

I firmly believe that the "curriculum" for the early years of faith, through at least Confirmation and Bar Mitzvah, is that God is love and that God loves us. The golden rule is nested in this truth.

If diversity and complexity frighten us, we will communicate that message to our children. If we do not personally know the love of God for us, that message will show to our children. If that love is known by us, that message will also show to our children. If we enjoy the diversity of origins in our family, that message is likewise transparent.

The children know that their parents are "two things" instead of just one. They are much more worried about whether the "likes of them" can be accepted in the world than whether God is one. If God or Mom and Dad disapproves of them, their chances for acceptance are less good. If God is approving, like Mom and Dad, theological differences intrigue them more than bother them.

The spiritual wealth we want for our children is the wealth of God's love for diversity. Fundamentalism denies that wealth. We believe this appreciative response to God's love for everyone is their spiritual inheritance.

Because as interfaith people we are pioneers, we know that we could be making a terrible mistake. Not every evolutionary development succeeds. Some developments are genuine errors, and some go on to be useful to others. The errors most parents make are the errors of the biblical Martha. We overwork, overworry, overfunction, and overdo. We go beyond the weight our bodies can carry. We get caught in the question of whether we are right. We panic. These fears are based in religious errors.

The experts agree. They say that what children need is a sense of being "anointed" by their family's love. They don't need protection so much as anointing. Overprotective mothers fail not only to protect but actually to make afraid. If Mom sees trouble everywhere, there must be a lot of trouble. If the house is not neat, then Mom looks worried. If the house can't be managed, then Mom also looks out of control. Children need to think their parents are in control — which is the main reason parents need to be good actors and teach children about paradox. Paradox is a trick by which we can seem to be in control of our nests even though we are not. If Mom can find a little peace and a little safety, maybe there is safety.

Susan B. Anthony spent ten days in jail in 1858 for voting when women were not allowed to vote. They say her husband was home with the children and that he had a terrible toothache. Knowing of this account allows me to worry less about the Yom Kippur catastrophe. Sometimes we can carry more than we can carry. By the help of God. But we should carry more than we can for only as long as we have to, not a second longer.

What is good about living in real time, as opposed to the kind of time that is supposed to be, fundamentalist time, is that a lot of the strange things that are happening become things that are supposed to be happening. This rearrangement of religious sensibility — from perfectionism to reality — is characteristic of a family that has escaped fundamentalism.

Fundamentalism tries to control things that can't be controlled. It offends life. We may be "out of control" from time to time. Every now and then it is wonderful to panic or to haul off and scream at a child. That shows that we have feelings. That we have limits. That we aren't perfect. I like screaming in the parking lot rather than at home. In the parking lot, there is lots of space for the noise to carry and it alerts the other people that you aren't perfect either. The next time they find enough security to scream at their children they'll remember you and be grateful for your leadership.

The point of this silly confession is to include the possibility of being wrong or stretched too far in almost everything you say about religion. God is large. God is not counting on us to control things. God does not love our self-righteousness so much as God loves our righteousness. Righteousness is faithful relationship with a loving God, not being right about God.

I don't want to be too harsh on fundamentalists without admitting to their impulse within myself. I too would love to bother God with pettiness while being right about everything. I just can't pull it off. I understand the urge to have a

rock-type faith. I relate with great joy, in fact, to some Pentecostals who combine great security with great flexibility and
joy in worship. What I don't care for in the fundamentalist
spirit is their hatred of those who don't agree. I join a loving
God in not tolerating that.

I remember standing with my seven-year-old daughter
waiting for a train. She pulled a disgusting pink wad out
of her mouth and said, "Ma, hold this." It was gum. There
was a tremendous intimacy in her request. Imagine letting me
hold her gum. The Martha in me said, Of course, I would be
glad to hold your gum. Can I polish your shoes while I'm
at it? The Mary in me said, You have to be kidding. Can't
you see I'm enjoying a few deep thoughts and don't want
to be bothered with your gum? The mother in me bridges.
She becomes functional on behalf of peace. No, I don't want
to hold your gum. You hold your gum. Or throw it away.
I don't exist to hold your gum. But if you like, I'll get a
wrapper for it and you can figure out what to do with it next.

I can imagine a mother mismothering by holding too
much gum, and I can imagine a mother mismothering by
holding too little. That's why we need both Mary and
Martha, and a Margaret as their composite: then we can
make more balanced mistakes. God is Margaret-like with us,
sometimes Mary and sometimes Martha, but mostly showing us the size of both, plus grace. God loves us well, not
permissively, not in a way that produces dependence, not in
a controlling way.

Martha, you will remember, was always doing things for
others; Mary sat at Jesus' feet and calmly listened. Neither
will do when faced with a wad of gum. To be a Margaret-
type mother, or father for that matter, one neither afraid of
work nor enslaved to work, it is important to know what
we want our children to be when they grow up. To know

where all this balance is heading. We want them to be safe in the village — and that requires that they be safe at home. We want them to be so well nested that they can fly away. We want them to carry the love of God with them; that will make them spiritually rich.

The great psychologist Carl Jung said that whatever we want our children to be, we should become ourselves. Any fault we find in our children we should rout out in ourselves. If we want Margaret-like children, we should become Margarets ourselves.

We raise our children through our bodies, which is to say, we raise our children through our souls. We are not either but both, soul-bodies or body-souls. Our goal is Margaret — who is perfect, but also imaginary. Our goal is family/village or village/family — not a perfect blend so much as a shifting one, and one capable of shifting with grace. Our goal is to worship God, as God truly is, beyond even the capacity of our multiplying paradoxes to contain her.

We learn most of the important things we know in our homes. If we can't tell the kids the truth about life there, we will probably not be able to tell them the truth at all. They will be led to live phony lives in phony homes. One of the big truths of smaller and larger worlds is imperfection. Things are *not* perfect, here or there.

I'll never forget the head deacon of one of our small rural churches. She was the kind of woman who wore her apron to meetings. Unfortunately, her minister was convicted of being a bigamist. When, as area minister, I visited with her and the Board of Deacons on behalf of the United Church of Christ, I suggested that "we have a problem." She responded with these important words. "We all have trouble in our families." She meant every word. Her church was not about to fire their minister because they loved him, bigamy and all.

"It takes a whole village to raise a child." This famous African saying puts our homes in their proper place. They raise children to truth, to paradox, to imperfection, but they have genuine limits. Not everything can be taught in or by the home. The nest is not perfect. There are some things we have to fly off to see and to know. God may be one of those. We *need* churches and synagogues, schools and malls to help us teach our children about life. We can't raise our children alone.

The village is the larger body of the family, and the family is the larger body of the mother or father. Alone our bodies are inadequate for motherhood much less Margarethood. Connected, covenanted, held together by baling twine, glue, love, the grace of God, and lots of luck, we are capable of growing our children "up." Unconnected — or, worse, convinced that everything is up to "me" and me alone — we haven't a prayer at raising our children. Not even the best nest will do.

It takes a whole village to raise a child. It takes companionship with a large God to bring a child into a rich religious inheritance. I grew up in a village on the banks of the Hudson River. It was the kind of place where people left you alone if you felt like dancing and skipping. I could stand in the street and sing my favorite song, "Zippety Dee Doo Dah," at the top of my lungs and no one would bother me for hours.

Villages should respect our privacy. When we say it takes a whole village to raise a child, we don't mean socialism. Or intervention. Or crossing the boundaries of private space. We mean enough civilization to protect private space, enough village surrounding the nest so that when the children fly, they have somewhere good to go.

What interfaith families need from the village is a little

more respect. A little less judgment. A little more appreci-
ation for what we are trying to do. We know we frighten
some of the village elders. They are there to be frightened.
They guard traditions and tribes and many do so well. But
as much as they are there to be frightened, we are there
to frighten them. We need their tradition; they need our
experimentation — if any of us are to find God.

John Updike talks about why he loves New England so
much. He says it's because of the respect people have for
each other's solitude. I don't know a mother who doesn't
need respect for her solitude. Or for the blessing out she is
giving a child in a grocery cart. That is very much her business. Likewise the joy she takes in something funny that just
happened. Great villages border, protect, and strengthen our
solitude. Great homes do the same thing.

I love my children the most just after I've come back from
some time away from them. Then, with the reset eyes of
the village, I can actually see them. Before time away from
them, especially if I've seen too much of them, they look like
bouncing blobs to me.

God keeps distance from us in the way a good parent
does. God makes sure we are not scared to be alone, even
with inadequate theologies, cosmologies, Christologies, and
the like. (I have been accused of such inadequacies just this
week. Thank God for standing close while others shoot ar-
rows, and thank God for taking off and giving me the room
to think as well.)

When I first had children, I assumed I would make our
nest into a fortress of protection against the village's mad
intrusions. I was never going to take my children to Disney
World. I wanted purer children. As a result of my early put-
downs of mass culture, my children adore franchise food. By
acting as though I was better than the street, I gave the street

a little victory. I should have known better since I too was raised by a fundamentalist. Just a different kind.

We take epic journeys and discover epic distortions. Not only is Disney World too far and too big, but it also teaches people like you and me — "Americans" we're called — that we deserve far and big. I see no way my nest can protect my children from becoming like their culture. All it can do is receive them back after they've gone "out."

Sometimes our best nest is not enough to protect our children from the rough. We have failed our children in so many ways that it takes courage to baptize them. Franchised food at every turn means that even when they spend their allowance it goes to make some big corporation rich and faraway villages poor. To name them in the name of Father, Son, and Holy Ghost takes courage — so poor are their choices. Maybe that's another reason we add blessings as interfaith people: we want to maximize their choices of getting to the right God.

Good but not perfect parents know where we stop and God starts. We can fly worms in for as long as we can manage, but eventually those little birds are going to spread their wings and jump straight out of the nest and, we hope, fly. God flies worms in to us precisely so that we can feed the children.

We raise our children with God and to God. Our nests are made of small and fragile sticks, little scraps of old feathers, string, and bark. Our world and our God is made from stiffer stuff, like love and trust, held as a foundation in open hands.

Chapter Five

Religious Experience as Religious Authority

We can know God by tradition. Or experience. Or reason. Or all three. I prefer the combination and the blend. That's why I, who love Jesus the Christ, married a Jew, who doubts that Jesus is Christ. His religious authorities and mine collide. They have had so many wars that the blood is everywhere. Auschwitz is one name in this fraternal war. The battle is about whose spiritual source is better. It is an underground war most of the time — although sometimes it surfaces in guerrilla activity at our kitchen table.

Humility works for peace in this war. It is also the best religious authority. The more humble and more loving people are when expressing their faith, the more likely it is authentic. The more swords they have in their hands or words, the less likely it is authentic. The Chinese sage was right: "Those who know the eternal do not speak of it, and those who do, don't." Surely, there are people who believe their own faith is so true that they can't imagine others living without it. Because of love they try to convince others of their

80

singular truth. There are such people — but more of the certain ones lose humility and love on their way to truth. Being right becomes more important to them than being loving, and those of us who count ourselves among the "uncertains" often become their victims. (Yes, we "uncertains" can also be imperial about our uncertainty.)

In an interfaith family, there is often a collision of well-established religious authorities — *and* an inner collision about what constitutes religious authority in the first place. In both of these collisions, humility and love war with pride and disrespect of the other.

When people do not ascribe religious authority to an established tradition and also do not have the chutzpa to be Sheila — their own individual and personal authority — those people face questions of religious authority. We inter-marrieds live this dialogue intimately and publicly at the same time. An example of how this works for us is in what we call "The Battle of the Worldviews." I may say that everything is going to turn out all right, and he may say the same thing. My faith is often based in the future; his in the past. My hope is often based in a serious, death-dueling transformation; his in becoming more right, following God more obediently.

In our battle he insists I am overly pessimistic and (his favorite word) "apocalyptic." I insist that he is overly pessimistic and "cynical." I don't see his hope; he doesn't see mine. I consider his hope insufficiently strong to wage war with my despair. He sees mine the same way. If Jesus did not die on the cross and rise on the third day, of course, my transforming pushes would be unreliable. My favorite definition of the gospel (from Canadian theologian John Douglas Hall) is that it is the permission and commandment to enter difficulty with hope. We go into a kind of tomb; we come out of a kind of tomb. That's how hope works. It works by transformation. (Or so my tribe taught me.)

Warren's hope is much less dialectical or fluid. For him, what we do is get deeper into the sphere of God's histori-cal activity. We move from disobedience to obedience. We become more ourselves or more our "better" selves. I often don't have the energy for that all alone. I need the help of Christ — and thus lean on the faith of the cross, which transforms me.

Warren almost never has the courage of the tomb. Of course, we surprise each other. I have seen him transformed overnight in response to the suggestion of a doctor; I have stuck on a point so insistently that it is he who prays, "Pry her off dead center." Still, the authorities by which we know God are fundamentally different. The historical narratives that shaped us bent us in different directions: we see these twists and turns in small and large familial discussions.

One is not better than the other so much as thoroughly different from the other. When we fight, as couples do, we fight the battle of the worldviews. I advocate change or im-mersion in the difficulty as gateway to renewal. He advocates more and deeper and better of the same.

These differences don't carry over to the religious activi-ties of prayer and thanksgiving. People of any faith can find a way to praise and thank the same God. Oddly, theology rarely causes wars in grace at the table.

A simple hands grace, from the children's first Sunday School, suffices to praise the nameless for our food and our evenings. "God be above us. God be below us. God be inside us. God be all around us. And God be with our friends." There are hand motions, pointing up, down inside, and — my favorite — all around. These motions are the prayer. They refuse to name God the way breath refuses to name

God; they are part of the Jewish tradition of God being more than a name.

Sometimes what happens next is a long theological conversation about who our friends are. This is the Jewish part. I find the dialogue most amusing. Usually one of the kids will offer that so and so may once have been a friend but is no longer.

Even better, though, is the surety of the announcement that if one family member is absent, he or she gets named. This peace lets me travel. I know they will remember me at home over their hamburgers, the way I might remember them over mine. The grace is simple, as graces should be. Its motion is its motion. I don't need the name of Jesus, but I am desperate for the sense of motion which comprises my faith. Warren's sturdiness is exemplified in the words — which is probably why we taught them to the children in the first instance.

We are trying not to fight. We are blending. We are mixing. We are experimenting. We are leaning on our different authorities of experience and reason and tradition to know the same God. We are a Jewish historian and a Christian apocalyptic: the one believes in a radical eternal, the other in a radical discontinuity. Both may tell the story of God. I would be lying if I said this battle of the worldviews is easy. It is not. It is often horrifying. What we think about God and where God can be found is such a life-forming pattern that intimates can find plenty to quarrel about. When our paths diverge, we are oddly on our own with our God. We are out in left field while our friend is out in right field, defending our God. Alone. Civil war has broken out in intimate quarters.

Would these isolations cause me to recommend that we marry our "own kind"? No. That would be too easy. God would be shrunk. But are different authorities among intimates hard on the intimacy? Yes. Harm is not done to God; oddly we search more vigorously for God when we differ with our best friend on where God can be found. But it is hard to remain friends without constant confirmation of one's worldview. The very absence of that confirmation can help religious authority along; we must develop our own spiritual and intellectual muscles. In the nearly constant self-explanation that occurs within an interfaith marriage, a new authority develops that is both dialogical and independent.

Religious authority is aided by the modesty afforded it by knowing that God speaks differently to different people. When someone we love and respect constantly emerges in a different place, we have no choice but to reverence that place. It is not us. It is different. It is genuinely different.

We become religious open-endedness — right but not completely right. This open-endedness, this lack of a closed universe, this door at the bottom of our heart, becomes our religious authority. It is not relativism; what happens in interfaith settings is not relativism at all. It is instead the nearly constant and flawed move to win points for your side. To show the virtue and benefit of transformation over continuity, for example. We fight for these values because we believe in them. We fight intimately, not on a soapbox. The opening in our heart, our cosmos, our worldview gets rubbed raw — and it also lets in the wind. It scabs over from time to time only to get rubbed raw again. Like Wendell Berry says about marriage itself, it is the willingness to get lost in the forest and the necessity to go out into the clearing again. Even after you have become afraid of the light.

I must complicate this matter one step further. Not all Christians are transformational and not all Jews continuous in their approach to God. We can find different experiences within our own traditions as well.

Jim Forbes of the Riverside Church in New York City tells a joke about his father riding an airplane. "Do you really believe this thing can fly and hold you up?" "I'll tell you the truth, son, I never did put all my weight down on that plane." When religious authorities war intimately, we become blessedly and mercifully incapable of putting all our weight down on our own certitude.

Downeast Mainers tell us that if you want to sink fast you should hang on to the anchor. And that is how I feel about my Christ. I never thought Jesus would want me to hang on too tight. That's the gospel I hear from him, consistently. We can have what we can let go of. We can be rich if we can be poor. We give to get. We lose our life to gain it. We relinquish, not hold. My Jesus would never throw his name around pompously.

From him derives my very absolute faith in letting go and being open, in not putting my weight down too fully anywhere. The gospel, at least my little kernel of it, is the freedom to float. And float I do.

These fluid religious authorities compel me to connection and activity in the larger world. The poor women in Guatemala who are advocating closer links between rural producers and urban consumers are me. We are the same process. That's why I invested (and lost) a lot of money in their farm operation. I did it for myself. I did it for my God. What was the authority? My sense of them as me, my sense that the peace of Jerusalem was my peace, that the polis was personal.

In these politics that keep things close, I invite a deliberate simplicity, self-reliance, self-provisioning. I can't imagine that Warren could do otherwise. There is a radical individualism to interfaith living; there is also a radical connection. We represent a new kind of *oikonomia,* the Greek word meaning household management from which both "ecumenism" and "economy" are derived. Opening God opens everything. The authority of my faith is my heart's sense of the other. When that is alive in me, I am alive to the one I know as Christ. When that is dead in me, I am dead to the one I know as Christ.

Church has not always contained God for me. Synagogue has not always contained God for Warren. Many of our friends experience the same thing: God has escaped religious authorities and religious institutions. More often, God has been in the streets, or the garden, or the hallways, or literature. God has been in laughter and liberations, like skipping the meeting that was pompously discussing God. But God has never been "not there."

Both church and temple have an awful habit of shrinking God to the legitimation of their own authority. While I want these institutions to have as much authority as possible, I want their authority to have the ping of good crystal. I long to report more experiences of good sound; instead, my experience has taught me the thud of plastic or heavy glass. No doubt this "door at the bottom of my heart" is a last resort. I didn't go there because I wanted to go there to find God. I went there because I couldn't quite believe all the church told me. When I went looking for God in my own experience, I was not disappointed. God was everywhere — but saying something that contradicted a good bit of the church's authority. The church did not have the only story. It had a good one — but it was not the only one.

I know that my fluidity is directly related to the fundamentalism of my youth. It grounded me enough to fly. Today 346 million Pentecostals on the planet fly with the same energy. They are wildly personal and sure of their own Holy Spirit — and they read their Bible rigidly. Structure and flight are deeply connected as religious authorities. Because of my excellent religious background — its "fundament" — I have religious ground, religious equity. I had the luxury of being born before the foundations shook hard enough to shake Reformation understandings of God. I still love the old hymns that praise the old God, but I love them humbly.

Religious authority comes from reason and experience and tradition. Reasoning through my experience as I stand in left field and my best friend stands in right has often brought me to God. Surely religious institutions have also brought me to God. I have asked God more than once how long I have to stay in the institutional church that often drives me nuts and makes me feel like I am doing "hospice work" in the UCC. The answer has this odd ring. "Seventy times seven." It is the same answer Jesus gave when asked how often we have to forgive our neighbor. I have been given too much by the church to let it go now. Seventy times seven is a trick answer. It means forever.

Mostly, for me, authoritative knowledge of God comes in experience at the open door. God comes as we pass through.

Dual and sometimes dueling authorities are not easy for children to comprehend. Surrounded as they and we are by an orthodoxy of monotheism — that God is one — interfaith children are more convinced than most children that their parents are religiously quirky. Most children have not figured out how much they need God and so are prepared to be religiously unimpressed. We are laying foundations for the future; we are not converting our children for today. Later they will need the God about whom we tell them now.

Children should be raised slowly and developmentally when it comes to religion. We should be as interested in their present as we are in their future. But most religious questions, including interfaith matters of authority, are simply not matters of concern for children. They are living spiritually, not religiously. They are concerned about basic acceptance, about trustworthiness. That means getting invited to the right birthday parties and counting on a parent to show up at 3:15 after saxophone lessons if that is what the parent said that he or she would do. Children's religious questions correspond to their developmental stages. They are not at generativity yet; they are still learning trust so that they may become generative later. Children are simply too small and too young to bear the freight of the big questions that are on our theological table and will eventually also be on theirs.

For example, my children have learned more of God and Spirit from the eighth puppy than they have from Torah, Testament, or Sunday School. For three weeks, we marveled at seven golden retriever puppies, born to Lilly one Sunday morning in July. Although we didn't know it at the time, she had actually given birth to eight. Lilly, only two years old herself, dropped one, probably the first, at the far edge of our property and left it there for the flies. She returned to the house to deliver the other seven in the basement. Two neighborhood kids came by and found the abandoned puppy, complete with umbilical cord. They tried to flag down passing cars. The would-be Samaritans who stopped on Route 116 South in Amherst refused to do anything about the discovery, assuming the obvious, namely, that the dog was a goner.

We learned later that a woman in a wheelchair came by on the sidewalk and took another approach. She found a place for the dog with an eleven-year-old up the hill, Zack Keenan. Zack waits with Isaac for the bus. He kept the dog alive with baby bottles of enriched formula on the advice of a Connecticut vet, a friend of his father.

When we put up our sign saying, "Golden Puppies for Sale," Zack came across the street with our eighth puppy, now named Merwyn, which went straight to Lilly's "extra" nipple.

My kids learned that no matter how lost we are, we can be found. If the children ever think that God has lost them, they can remember Merwyn and understand that for just a while, he had lost God, only to be found by one of God's messengers — in the person of Zack.

In addition to the home schooling provided by lost puppies, dead goldfish, and the like, we teach our children the catechism in Confirmation preparation and the Torah in Bar and Bat Mitzvah training. Many have found life-long comfort from the memorization of the Heidelberg catechism. "What is your only comfort in life and death?" "That I belong — body and soul, in life and in death — not to myself but to my faithful savior Jesus Christ." Heidelberg tells Merwyn's story with words.

Imperfect parents "luck" into eighth puppies all the time. We have nonstop educational moments for the word of God. We home theologians simply need to connect the dots. What does a lost but found puppy tell us about God? Exactly what a young child wants to know in the supermarket. If I get lost, Mom or Dad will come and get me. They'll find me. Religious authority is religious experience!

The psychologist Anna Freud, daughter of Sigmund, claimed that a good-enough parent was better than a perfect parent. This long spectrum of activity between "good" and "perfect" is a tremendous difficulty for parents. We can join God in wondering whether to expect too much or too little from our creations. When parents expect too little from our children, we harm as much as when we expect too much. Children become little kings and queens in the realm of self-esteem. They don't learn piano, or soccer, or Confirmation; they assume they are fine just the way they are. Their muscles go unused.

Culture, and missing puppies, are sites for learning about God — but not all experience is going to be holy. (The day after Isaac's Bar Mitzvah he snuck into an R-rated movie.) We have to be experience sleuths. We have to pay lots of attention to our children's lives. When something happens, we need to incorporate it into our family prayer. That prayer will become their religious authority: it will be right as a rite. They will use it as a pathway to God when they need to.

In addition to prayerful watching of experience, there are many other simple ways we can develop religious authority in our interfaith homes. What follows are a dozen possibilities for good but not perfect parents, for those who want to transform culture into its original created purposes. These are authoritative guideposts for spiritually rich children. Each depends on the authentic religious authority of our experience with our children.

Jesus was never a parent. Thus he did not have to deal with the fierce "mother bear" love of a mother or father. He knew more about agape than he did about married love or blood love. But what he knew makes sense in the context of family: there is the need for absolutely unconditional love that has conditions, limits, and boundaries in its expression. Without those boundaries, children aren't really loved. Spouses aren't loved. They are instead endangered.

The authority that enables children to know God is experiential authority; they are too young for tradition or dogma. That's why, first of all, we prepare the ground for religious authorities in our homes by focusing on the family's continuity, not its fragmentation. Show that you mean the lines about "better and worse, richer and poorer, till death do us part." Speak often of their births and beginnings and of how we will all be together as and when we die. Pay lots of attention to the dying, visit the elderly and the sick to make sure that children see the long line of life. Thus, they will know about family continuity — which directly transforms the short attention span of modern culture. Thus they will be ready to love tradition and its authorities.

A second way to help religious authority along in the home is to make sure people eat together. Every religious tradition mediates God's presence in and through food. We have to be very careful in modern culture not to let God come out of a paper bag, the contents of which are eaten alone. Eat at least one meal together every day, even if you have to eat at nine o'clock at night. Make it a family rule. Let eating be a daily act of celebration: the children will see and know what you are doing. Abraham Joshua Heschel speaks often of the "sense of glory in daily acts of celebration."[32] Eating can be just eating or it can be a daily act of celebration.

Culture does not give eating together much support these days. For Barbara Dafoe Whitehead the model of family relationships is based on "unfettered market choice, limited warranties, and contingent obligations."[33] Nonbinding, short-term interactions are the focus of our public life; they are increasingly the pattern of our private life. Even if you buy take-out, put in on a plate. Don't eat out of paper bags. And if you have to eat out of a paper bag, put a tablecloth on the table. Whatever you do, make the meal an absolute necessity. If you can't do it daily, do it weekly. Bring the fragments together. Food is religious experience.

Abraham Joshua Heschel understood his life mission as the piety of a living Judaism. Piety is eating and praying and thanking God. Piety is the normalization of religious authority. Piety is experiencing religion in a regular way on a regular basis, in what theologian Ada María Isasi-Díaz calls *lo cotidiano,* everyday things. Piety is the daily experience of religious authority.

Religious authority is aided by giving thanks before eating. A family that prays together does stay together. It's not just a slogan. The best prayers are the memorized ones that are repeated over and over again. Children take these with them in their heart. They are the way they remember their family. If there is time and relaxation sufficient to manage it, asking each member of the family to give thanks for one good thing that happened in their day will go a long way to create the kind of community children need to thrive. (It also helps us experience sleuths.) Prayer transforms culture and prayer transforms people.

Third, we may also talk about bad things, early and often. If someone moves away, or a teacher gets sick, or a goldfish dies, talk about it. Jews swear that the people who move into the river find the waters parting before them.

Edna St. Vincent Millay wrote, "Childhood is the kingdom where nobody dies... nobody that matters, that is." Children need practice learning that loss and death do not separate us from the love of each other or the love of God. Nothing separates us: that is the message we need to teach our children.

Fourth, we need to see our marriages as a display of religious experience to our children. One of the genuine arenas of difficulty is marriage — which is not news to children. Do not be surprised if marriage is a difficult commitment. Struggle with it. Don't hide the struggle: children see. Some couples use in-house separations quite effectively, thus ritualizing their marriage and keeping the double-rent problem at bay. Others take sabbaticals from each other for short periods. Don't be naive. The "real" arrangements of culture are against marriage and family. Those arrangements are for the disposable and the intentionally obsolescent, what Wendell Berry calls "human trash." Every wife and every husband knows it.

Fifth, do not underestimate your enemies. Mary Pipher realizes that families are no longer so much in difficulty internally but are rather under external assault.[34] We are targeted markets. We work too long and too hard to pay our mortgages and insurance. We live in a family-unfriendly economic order, which nevertheless wants us to feel guilty for not living the lives of the family-friendlier economies in which we were raised. To transform the culture that hurts our families is the obvious antidote to the problems families face.

> In the past when therapists saw troubled teenagers, they could generally assume that the parents had problems. That's because most teenagers were fine. Troubled teens were an exception and required some explaining. Today most teenagers are not fine. At one time we helped kids differentiate from enmeshed families. Now we need to help families differentiate from the culture.... In our current world it is almost impossible not to be an over-anxious parent.... The anxiety that parents feel or their children is not neurotic, it is realistic.[35]

Sixth, we may work for a family economy and paycheck that requires a total of only sixty hours of work a week or thirty hours a week for a single parent. When working women and men experience the double bind of always supposed to be someplace else, they are correct in their self-assessment. What families really need is to end the two-career family, the double workplace, the eight-hour day.[36]

Seventh, try to live within a schedule that is family-friendly. Time is such a priority that we dare not keep God out of it. What does God want us to do with our time? That is the important family question.

Eighth, make sure to give away as much money as possible, hopefully a tithe, and make sure the children know this is what you do with "our" money. Families need to make sure children can see and know God in the uses of money in the home.

Ninth, find a way to praise your children that is truthful. We often believe that praising our children will improve their self-esteem. But aimless flattery is worse than useless; it teaches children that they can slip by. Careful praise does not mean that we don't say positive things. Instead, we say truthful ones. We take religious aim at hypocrisy. Nick Stinnett and John De Frain tell us:

> Strong families have certain things in common...
> appreciation, open communication, time together, a
> commitment to promoting happiness, spiritual welfare
> and a way to cope effectively with stress.... In a strong
> family, we hear 20 positive comments for every one
> negative comment.[37]

These positive comments are not necessarily about each other or related to self-esteem. They are positive about the world and life and interactions, not worried or anxious about how we don't have enough. In most families today, the vernacular is insufficiency. Hurry, move, must go now. Transform the family vernacular: there is enough.

Tenth, once a week, take your children one by one to a breakfast or on a drive or a walk. Religious authority is aided by confidence and solitude, by genuine one-on-one connection. Each child needs times that are free, "in which grades, chores, rule violations and money are not even mentioned. Rather, parent and child can just visit."[38]

Eleventh, pray for your children. Pray for them by name. Initiate a Sabbath dinner on Friday nights or a Sunday lunch in which each child is touched and blessed, the way Jews do it in normal observance of Sabbath.

Twelfth, lighten up. God is with us as we raise our children!

Chapter Six

Institutional Lag

Religious institutions have had to revise themselves on more than one occasion in American life. I think of the 1950s, when religion became child-centered as baby boomers were born in large numbers. Or of Jonathan Edwards being fired from his church in Northampton because, as his biographer puts it, there was no longer land for the parents to parcel to keep their children home. Edwards was let go because he "failed to reach the children."

Demographics and political economies shift and so do religious institutions. The historical fact that the rise in capitalism gave birth to the Protestant Reformation makes us quiver: we have no doubt that an economic change of similar size is occurring right now in globalization. Surely God will again bring forth a new revelation.

Simultaneous with globalization, religious distinctions continue to be blurred. Catholics, Jews, and Protestants are more alike and thus have even more in common than, say, in 1950. Then their boundaries were clear; one could tell a Catholic from a Protestant from a Jew. Today it is not so easy. (I am waiting for a new category on the census form: "blend.") Moreover, the conversation within each movement is very similar: How do we keep the young in the fold? Be-

cause one was born Jewish or Catholic or Protestant does
not mean that one will stay so. Simply because many children are born with a mixed heritage, there is considerable
membership shifting between the three groups. Finally, the
three groups have similar internal tensions: the traditionalists and the modernists are in hot and heavy conversation.
The only place where the orthodox and the progressives war
more is in Israel itself. The traditionalists in each movement
have more to say to each other than the modernists: one
prefers the good old days; the other has left them behind.

Changes in the modern economy — notably the two-career
family, increased demands on workers, the loss of benefits,
and the need for most people to work more than one regular job — have had a profound effect on the voluntary
character of all religious institutions. They can't get free
help (usually women's), and thus are in a scramble for labor themselves to keep their volunteer-based organizations
going. These social, cultural, and economic shifts underlie
the blending of the constituency of each faith. Ethnic and
class differences remain, with identifiable attributes. But it is
a grievous social mistake to automatically assume the religious faith of an "apparent" member of one of these groups.
There is a strong possibility that the person belongs to none
of these formerly dominant groups, but is instead a Moslem,
Buddhist, "New Age," or is unaffiliated, even if the person looks for all reasonable purposes like a Jew or an Irish
Catholic.

In this interesting context of simultaneous blur and globalization, we hear the word "boundary" everywhere, precisely
when the boundaries are rapidly changing. The more borders
people cross, the more we hear about boundaries and their
proper maintenance. The word is used anxiously because the
fences are down. People feel "mushed" about and don't quite

know what to expect or when to expect it. The very breaking down of the barriers is part of the fountain and fundament of the Judeo-Christian tradition. Oddly, we are wringing our hands over our success. We wanted to welcome the stranger! Yet, the broken borders add to the sense of being stranded or orphaned that many interfaith families feel: there is no institutional home for us, yet.

Institutions work on establishing clear identities, developing appropriate niches for their faith, becoming clear and well bounded — precisely as the political economy and personal lives of people blend. Presbyterians join all the rest in putting out videos on "what it means to be a Presbyterian" long after people have lost interest in that question. The faith communities still have the vessel but not the theology to carry the people. The people have moved on to a God that is no longer Presbyterian.

I think of Jesus on the subject of boundaries. He made it clear that he was the "Lord of the Sabbath," implying that religious boundaries were not a matter of concern to him. He made it clear that family boundaries of blood were less important to him than those of love, thus confusing the matter of boundaries and blood relations. He wryly suggested that we give to Caesar what belongs to Caesar and that we give to God what belongs to God, as though it were easy to determine the differences. He also spoke of welcoming the stranger into our home — as though there were no difference between intimates and strangers. In many ways, Jesus was not personally well bounded. He crossed over lines of blood and class and religious authority. He did so not to hurt others or take from them but to help them and give to them.

St. Paul also undermined religious boundaries: he constantly advised people not to be too beholden to those who wanted circumcision. In Christ, "circumcision is nothing,

and uncircumcision is nothing; but obeying the commandments of God is everything" (1 Cor. 7:19). Paul's new
creature is bounded by God, not by religion. Our "high
priest" is a minister of "the true tabernacle, which the Lord
pitched, and not man" (Heb. 8:2, KJV). Likewise, the law
is written in our hearts, not in stone (Heb. 8:9–13.) God
breaks boundaries. In the modern synthesized communities,
there is the odd hunch teasing us, that God had these very
mixtures in mind. Cultural critic Trin Min Ha observes how
"thoroughly hybrid...things are. Other is between us, not
out there. Cultures are far from being unitary. We no longer
have clear borders. One constantly threads the fine line
between positioning and depositioning. One travels trans-
culturally while engaging in the local habitus which links
inhabitants."[39]

Theologian Chun Hyun-Kyung expresses a basic apprecia-
tion of the postmodern mixed-up-edness, which, I believe, is
the world that God has always seen. At the Auburn conference on the public vocation of women's theology, she teased
her detractors: "You don't like my syncretism but you do
like the syncretism of orthodox Christianity?" We can imagine God feeling the same way about orthodox Christianity
that St. Paul felt about the tabernacle of his time. In Christ
God broke the boundary between human and God, heaven
and earth, eternity and time. This should tell us something
about how God feels about boundaries.

Likewise the God of Israel sent the people out, not back.
When the Jews left Israel, they left it for a larger world.
In Diaspora, which continues until this day, Jews find a
home. The Jews are advised at least thirty times in the Torah
to "welcome the stranger into your midst." This border-
crossing stranger is mentioned even more than monotheism
or Sabbath. "Remember that you once were a stranger." You

crossed a border. You went far from home. Institutions try to create homes; faith creates homes for the homeless.

Boundaries between faiths are not eternal so much as practical. They give people a home in an otherwise unfriendly world. Institutions comfort our identities by supporting them with homes. We get a sense of belonging by worshiping in certain ways or by eating certain kinds of food. I think of souvlaki and borscht and tabouli. I think of the pride with which a Jewish mother teaches her children how to light the Sabbath candles. Or of a young Italian woman, on her way to work, with tears in her eyes as she watches an old Catholic woman, a little stooped, with black veil, coming from Mass at dawn with a missal in her hand. Or the way a Protestant makes cookie bars for the church bazaar — and does so with a sense that they are an ancient and generational bread. The particular cultures of these communities will last as long as the genetic postures and body shapes. These identities are delightful but they are not eternal. Rather, they are the stuff that makes institutions institutions: they are ethnic, cultural, psychological, and magnificent. But they are not divinely ordained fences. They do not need the protection of the divine to "save" them. Institutions are relative: the more fluid they are, the better.

I note now that my son Jacob often gets the fried rice from the Chinese outlet and the tacos from the Mexican outlet at the food court at the mall. I laugh at his plate, but I know what it means: that blend is basic to him.

We need institutional identities to make us feel safe and comfortable and real. We value these earthen vessels that hold treasure. But we dare not idolatrize or absolutize or imperialize them. They are just packages. They are not the goods; they hold the goods. While interfaith families often experience dismay about not having one place to go but several, we also gain comfort from knowing what is ultimate and what is not.

Wallace Stevens argued that we don't live in a place but in a description of a place. Institutions describe places for us to live in. They develop stories that tell us who we are. These "pictures" we have of each other draw us for each other even before we meet.

Then we meet. At many levels, we are very much the same. Still, we remain capable of profound differences and these differences are more likely to show up in intimate relationships. Even deeper in the nest, we turn out to be the same again. Just human, in a Christian way. Just human, in a Jewish way. There remain differences that affect intimate relations: the shelf life of a good stereotype is as long as the reach of history. Still, we have more world in common than history apart. The consistency of the environment of our religious institutions as we enter the twenty-first century means that we are, finally, much more alike than we are different. Blurred and blurring religious institutions will fight to preserve identity; they will also fail if they misunderstand the root commonality of people.

One of the things that we have in common is a joint sense of Exodus, of being uprooted, of being on our way after something significant is over and done with. In its statement on Uprooted People, the World Council of Churches challenges "churches worldwide to rediscover their identity, their integrity and their vocation as the Church of the Stranger." The year 1997 was designated the Year of Uprooted People. More than one in every fifty human beings is now a refugee or international migrant. One might say that the churches are catching up with the synagogues, long havens for immigrants in many lands. The uprooted face closed borders, closed hearts, and closed minds. The WCC document states:

> As churches, we lift up all these who are compelled by severe political, economic and social conditions to leave their land and their culture....Uprooted people are those forced to leave their community, those who flee because of persecution and war, those who are forcibly displaced because of environmental devastation and those who are compelled to seek sustenance in a city or abroad because they cannot survive at home.

Religious uprooting is different from that of the refugee, but they share some common characteristics. We are spiritually homeless in the way refugees feel physically homeless. Pearl Buck describes this condition well when she speaks of herself, the daughter of a Chinese missionary, as "capable of feeling homeless on both sides of the world."

I was astonished to read in the *New York Times* of a couple, like many, who shuttle between New York and Costa Rica. The words that Mr. Mateo used to describe his shuttle are precisely the ones I would use to describe my interfaith marriage: "I believe people like us have the best of two worlds. We have two countries, two homes. It doesn't make any sense for us to be either this or that. We're both. It's not a conflict. It's just a human fact." We may be both — but rare is the institution or neighborhood that will receive us that way. Yet.

We have only to remember our own families of origin to understand what this uprooting has meant. My great grandparents came from Scotland and Germany to America. Who knows where my children will go? My son swears he is going to outer space, and maybe he will.

When we open doors, we risk ethnic blending. We risk uprooting. We also risk becoming finally the church of the Stranger. We risk becoming "the Whole People of God," which is the name of a Protestant curriculum used by a growing ecumenical group of Christian Sunday School teachers.[40] We can count on people to develop the institutional resources we need; we can also count on some institutional lag.

In this stranger-filled spiritual context, institutions are far behind. Institutions have and need identities and loyalties, but people have spiritually and economically gone beyond brand loyalty. We shake and bake, mix and match, sift and blend. We take a little of this and a little of that, and we make ourselves as we go.

I find that what I know of God I often know after the fact — by showing up someplace before I know I am there. I was no longer spiritually at home in my denomination a long time ago. I had outgrown it. I had no hymns for my God nor liturgies save those written tomorrow. I had no marriage services or burial services save those of a shattering individuality. I knew with Abraham Joshua Heschel that the real issue for interfaith people is faith.[41] I knew that I joined Jews and Moslems in a common fight against secularists who thought there was no God. But religious institutions were actually warring with each other! In the words of Carl Braaten, a Lutheran theologian who longs for one church again, the tragedy of the Protestant Reformation is that we are counting the angels on the heads of each other's pins rather than developing an open and common faith.

While I longed for the full-voice choir of one church, all the songs were beyond it and not written yet. God was there, but not denominationally. God was still with me, but as Thou or Breath or Beyond or Mystery. I began to thank God every night that I had outgrown my church home. And then the pride caught up with me. I realized I had not outgrown God at all but that God had outgrown me.

I thanked God every night that I was a member of a church that really believes (sometimes) that "God has yet more light to shed upon humanity," in the famous words of Pilgrim John Robinson. I thanked God that I had married a Jew so I could see and know more than I could from the little place I was standing.

When it was time for both Confirmations and B'Nai Mitzvahs for my children, I had an urge to continue with Nigerian rites of passage and Asian meditations. Almost everything "institutional" seemed too small for the God to whom they were going. And it still does.

Notwithstanding these institution-busting claims, our scriptures clearly advise that we say and spread the name of Jesus. Our institutions are built upon a missionizing and missionary impulse. And our strength has come from these impulses. It seems to me that there are at least two kinds of evangelism: one has bad manners, the other does not. When the Southern Baptists held their annual convention in Salt Lake City and "evangelized" the resident members of the Church of Jesus Christ of Latter-day Saints, they were unwelcome. More precisely, the Mormons greeted them with a quiet and hostile graciousness. The Baptists "evangelize" every city they visit as a national body; their pride knows few bounds. They are typical of Christian institutions.

The evangelization of any city is rude, but the Mormon visitation was particularly rude. Mormons are one of the American religious groups who take their religion very seriously. Most American believers permit God to be a seventh or an eighth of their life; Mormons give their God a much higher rank. The Southern Baptists were particularly insulting when they insisted that the Mormons are not Christians, which they clearly say they are.

Self-definition is a good basis for religious etiquette. Who is one Christian to tell another Christian that the other is not a Christian? The Jesus Christ I worship would *never* have stepped on another's toes in this self-serving a way; instead, he would have asked the very important question, "Who do you say that I am?" Speak for yourself, says my Lord. Don't speak for others.

Not all evangelism has bad manners. Some is a genuine sharing from the heart of what we know as the "evangel" or the Messiah or the truth of our own small portion of a large faith. We can speak Christ softly or loudly. Spoken loudly, the very word "Christ" becomes the oppression that the genuine Christ liberates us from. We are not here to control each other, or the world, but to love each other. And love is different from control. Institutions, unfortunately, work for control. Control does give us homes and boundaries, but it is still control.

If I offer you what I know of God as a gift, I have the good manners of evangelism. If I offer you what I know of God as a club, I have the bad manners of evangelism. The difference is control. The gospel is an action by God that refuses control. The gospel is an action of love and gift.

The Southern Baptists were telling the Mormons that Baptists are superior. They tried to "improve" the Mormons. This behavior is not evangelism; it is control. Religious control is no prettier than political or social control. It is bad manners, and it is un-Christlike. We need Christlike institutions, with good manners, in the global age. We have a few but not enough.

A friend tells the story of the Reformation theologians Calvin and Zwingli. They are on their way to a major confrontation over the directions of their separate movements and are to visit the very next day. Zwingli dreams that two goats are circling two mountains. Ambling. Walking in a deep calm. All of a sudden it becomes apparent that their paths are not only going to cross but that they are going to cross at a stretch in the mountain where the pass is narrow and only one will be able to go at a time. The goats continue on their way and, sure enough, they meet. One goat lies down and allows the other to walk through the pass. Then the goat gets up and continues on the journey initiated.

Zwingli wondered the rest of his life why his God's-eye view of the goat's passage never told him which goat was his. He feared that the passing goat might have stepped on the lying goat, but it did not. It passed by. I wonder if it said "Excuse me" as it passed.

Religious groups often think of truth as a contest in which one has to win and the other lose. But there is plenty of room on any mountain, in any city, for many groups to be somewhat right. They don't need to knock each other around or off the mountain.

They do need to give one another the gift of what they know about God. That's all. They don't need to win a contest but rather simply to share. That sharing is not small: it is large and it is enough.

Whether institutions can embody such openness and fluidity is another question, especially in a world where "niching" is all. I believe that if God wants earthen vessels for God's treasures, God will build them. Right now, we are in a period of hospice care for the institutions we have known and loved. When God is ready, new shapes will arrive.

For the moment, Catholics, Protestants, Jews, and more newly arrived American faiths will join the bishop of the

Church of South India, D. T. Niles, and argue that "evangelism is one beggar telling another beggar where to find bread."

While we wait for the new vessels to arrive, we can celebrate our faith together as best we are able. There is nothing wrong with the old forms — but they are a little tight fitting. We need a new wardrobe.

These institutional problems do strand interfaith families even more than they strand other kinds of families. We either double-time our children's religious development, or we make a choice for one home or another. Either choice can be good, especially when we realize that we are not facing any more or less institutional lag than other believers are. We are simply facing it from a different perch in a common wilderness. Economic, political, and cultural changes are making each of our faiths new.

Right now our culture is replacing religion with spirituality. Some of the new spirituality is "designer," expensive, ungodly, and self-serving, reminding one of nothing so much as a grand American advertising scheme. And some of it is alive and real and spirit-filled. Religions often help us to know the difference between the real and the phony by educating us to ways of thinking about texts and history. As religions become institutionally weaker, we will find a lot more phoniness. But we will have to wade through it all to find God, who is often a diamond in the rust.

Some of us find a way through these spiritual hazards by reverting to even more ancient names for God, names that transcend the centuries. *Sophia,* meaning wisdom, is an ancient name for Christ and is among the newest and most popular names for God. Jews use it because it predates Jesus. I was at a conference in Hungary of university chaplains from Eastern and Western Europe, and we could only worship in Latin. Otherwise people fought over the proper language and pronouns to use for God.

Zen wisdom tells us how we get through the many hazards: "By showing up, staying present, telling the truth, and being unattached to the outcome." Rabbi Hillel put the same advice a little differently: "If I am not for myself, who will be? If I am only for myself, what am I? If not now, when?" Sounds easier than it is. We stay with our institutions because we know we need institutions. We also keep our eye on them and try to pry them open. We live in them now. We try to live spiritual lives inside religious institutions. Religion is the package for spirituality.

Often people of color have an easier time than white people with spirituality. Marimba Ani offers a clue about why white people are spiritually depressed: "We have an apprehension of cosmic interrelationship.... We want anything that sets us apart." Many people of color see their safety, salvation, shalom in connection. Others often do not. Genuine spirituality can often be determined by whether it connects us with or isolates us from the rest of humanity, which the Judeo-Christian tradition has always argued is the site of God's activity. That God is here, among us, at work. Sometimes it is the hardest thing for white folk to know that. We thought we were in charge, not God. Individualism — and its dangerous lack of connections — is the enemy of institution. And without institutions religion has no package. People can't pick it up or touch it or use it to make identities.

Jews and Christians share an active God, one constantly packaging and making new things out of human history. Jews and Christians part at the incarnation, but both see God as active in history. Church is often figured as the "body of Christ," the continuing revelation of God in Jesus. If these activities in history are truly divine, then we simply have to wait for God to be active again and create a postdenominational denomination.

This matter of God being both close and far away, this matter of God showing up on earth, is not easy to understand. Institutions try but we fail. Kathleen Norris said she understood almost everything about Christianity except Christ: "I often felt a void at the center of things: Christianity with the center missing."[42]

Where Jews and Christians also part company about God in history is in the enormous subject called Christology, with its Trinitarian focus. Christians worship the Jewish God in toto and go on to add two more "persons." Norris uses the image of quark to explain her understanding of the Trinity. She appeals to the central notion of community and interrelationship within the Trinity and says that only quarks could show us the dance of such communal interrelationship at the heart of God. She shows us how God could be both very near and very far away. This everywhere God is very important to institutional thinking: we dare not alienate God from our institutions but rather must push institutions into godliness.

Some think that the image of the church as the body of Christ is much too exclusive. Instead, they prefer a more connected image, that the world, not just the church, is God's body. This image deepens the insight of the common creation story in a way that helps Christians to remythologize the relation of God and world for our time. Church, then, becomes an immature metaphor for world. Jews and Christians can part all they want — and no believer need worry. God is active in the world.

The Russian poet Yevtushenko claims that in the maternity ward in Baku the nurse switched the tags on the babies so the soldiers wouldn't know which were Armenian and thus wouldn't kill them. In this time of institutional lag, I would love to have the power to conduct a similar ecclesiastical experiment, simply switching people around at birth to see what happened.

The answers to big questions about the nature of God in our changing cultures will eventually yield less fuzzy answers than we have now. New and renewed institutions will develop around those ideas. From these ideas, then these institutions, will come rituals and liturgies, hymns and names for a shared God.

Between now and then, we wait on the Lord. We renew our strength. We mount up with wings like eagles. Oddly, we all carry the burden of waiting as though it was ours and ours alone. It is not. It is a burden we share.

According to the guarantee in the title of Alice Walker's book *Anything We Love We Can Save,* we can live without these institutions. We can save their wine and let go of their wineskins.

We can also live beyond the world-full-of-enemies precept that institutions use to build themselves up — and not only the Southern Baptists do this. "Once the whole world gets into NATO, we won't need to take any more of that crap from Mars," declared one pundit, demonstrating a very human habit of demonizing *something* as a way of saving ourselves. Institutions make enemies out of strangers to build themselves up; people of faith do not. But people of faith need institutions, and we need them to carry our faith authentically.

Chapter Seven

What Kind of Conflict Is Interfaith Conflict?

When members of interfaith families get pushed, we want to be right. We don't want to share the platform of correctness. Instead of saying yes or no, quietly, to each other's practice, we start treading on each other's toes with the words "right" and "wrong." "Yes, I can go to services with you today" and "No, I prefer not to" are very different from "I'm right" and "You're wrong." Still, many of us don't want to share the platform. If we can give up our defense of our faith and our family of origin, we can get along as well (or as badly) as other human beings do in intimate settings. We can become normal. If we cannot give up being right about God, a matter on which most people for most of history have wanted certainty, then, in addition to regular kinds of human sin and affliction, we have an additional difficulty. We war with our intimates over matters of right and wrong.

Many define racism as the denial of ordinary status. Many argue that we should stop "racing" each other and ourselves and dive to the depth of humanity that is shared. But if we did that, if we forswore labels and the historic freight they bear, what arguments could we use for being right?

Interfaith living teaches us to know strangeness as well as we know rightness. It teaches us the strangeness of ourselves; we live in a world where people learn their connection to their strangeness. If we all admit to being a bit strange, there is less room on the top of the pyramid for someone to be best and right. Letting go of being right is the prelude to being the children of God.

Harriet Lerner provides some suggestions about solving conflicts of this size.[43] One is self-focus as the best route to intimacy. Another is to renounce reactivity on behalf of activity. "Reactivity blocks self-focus" (205). A third is to become "less of an expert on the other and more of an expert on our self" (209). Interfaith families are strongly connected to this notion. We don't blend until we become fully ourselves and are given that kind of permission by the other. When Warren attends my church service, he does not receive communion. Nor does he expect me to reserve the name of Jesus so as not to offend his ears. When I attend Sabbath services, I do not understand all that is going on. I often complain that the services are too long and in a foreign language. (I have also been an advocate of brevity and the vernacular in my own communion!) But these matters are not "my business." I go as partner, not as participant.

Lerner also advocates an end to overfunctioning, which owes a lot of its source to being right or at least not being caught being wrong. She is not an advocate of under-functioning either — but advises functioning as the best one can for the self and for others. That means knowing our impact on the situation but not overdoing it. When we go into reactivity, all we see is the other. We blot out ourselves. Self-definition that says no to being right and yes to being is the challenge of interfaith living. We can refuse the temptation to be right and simply accept the challenge to be who we are, when we are, where we are.

I am reminded of the many ways we let other people tell us who we are. We wear approved clothes and make approved noises. We worship approved Gods and think approved thoughts. We indulge these patterns because we are dependent on other people's approval. Instead, we might live for God's approval: nowhere does the God beyond God recommend that some of us be right and others wrong. We can all be a little right and a little wrong, especially in the eyes of God.

In the common Bible that Jews and Christians share, there is an enormous advocacy on behalf of those called strangers. The texts number in the dozens: we are to welcome the stranger within our gates. People speak of the stranger as though they knew who he or she was. I have a suspicion about the stranger that scripture only metaphorically confirms. The stranger is us; the stranger is within us. One of the reasons "being right" is such a popular substitution for being is that it is easier to focus on others than on ourselves. It is exquisitely difficult to define ourselves and to be who we are.

While there are many texts which exclude this one or that one, biblical interpreters agree that strangers count in both first and second testaments. Likewise, the stranger "within" counts. God loves not only the normal or those on the inside: God loves the strange. God affirms the outsider, the one inside each of us and the ones genuinely outside our gates. God actually affirms what we don't know about ourselves or each other. God affirms and understands the way we are strangers to ourselves as well as each other. This knowledge makes me want to shout amazing grace; instead, I often refuse the grace and create trouble with myself and others. I go for the right instead of the strange, when going for the strange could save me. Flannery O'Connor said it all: "You shall know the truth and the truth shall make you odd."

Compounding the psychological fear of our own other-ness and the refusal to self-define, there is the environment of incredible movement in which we live. Ours is not a stay-at-home time. We put wheels on our feet and telephones in our pockets. We move around. Ours is not a quiet time. It is a moment of massive border crossing. People are going all over the world spiritually, even if only via their local book stores. Intermarriage as well as the ecumenism of the water cooler involve people in a nearly constant religious diversity. All this border crossing is about getting to our deeper selves as well as getting somewhere "outside of us." It also causes lots of conflict.

When we travel to strange and foreign lands, we also travel to strange and foreign inner lands. We find both enormous connection between people and enormous discon-nection. Yes, they do grill rats in the Bangkok market, and people do eat them and enjoy them. Yes, Americans do use up most of the ozone driving around all alone in automo-biles. Which is stranger, rats or cars? What is common is strangeness.

I interpret both testaments as understanding that there is a little of me in you and a little of you in me. There is a little of me in a criminal and a little criminal in me. There is a little of me in a saint and a little saint in me. We *are* they. You *are* I. We are not nearly as distant from each other as we imagine. Better put, Jews and Christians have more in common than not. The conflicts that we experience are less basic than we imagine.

When the law is summarized, its very summary is the purposeful confusion of the neighbor and the self. First we are to love God. Then we are to love our neighbor as we love our self. The neighbor is the naked one or the homeless one. Again, with Rabbi Hillel, we find an inversion of the golden rule, that I am not to do anything that I wouldn't want done unto me. The connectedness of one stranger to another is the theme of both the positively and negatively stated golden rule. This rule does not create conflict at all; it promotes peace. Nevertheless, it didn't take me long to get into a "conversation" with a Jewish friend about whether the positive or negative statement of the golden rule was "better."

I can imagine a conversation in which, instead of competing for the best morality, we self-define. Self-definition says where we are and what we think we follow and also leaves an opening, a caesura, a pause, a space in which, while we are being ourselves, others can be themselves.

A musician was asked why he could play the notes so well. He responded that it was not he playing the notes; the notes did that themselves. What he handled was the pauses between the notes: that was the tricky part. Interfaith conflict comes when we don't handle the pauses well, when we aren't quiet long enough for the other to show what the other wants to show us.

Interfaith families not only compete for correctness. We also compete over normality and legitimacy. Some of us see ourselves as "exceptional" and declare ourselves rare and beautiful. Others go the normal route. Either way, we are calling more attention to ourselves than we need. I can imagine "interfaith" living being much more normal than people think it is. I covet the day when my type of family is invisible.

I think of my own Missouri Synod family of origin. The approved thought was that we were all of one faith in one family. But my aunt was married to a Jew, and my mother's best friend was married to a Catholic. The historical reality is more interfaith than most people even notice.

Interfaith conflict is intimate. It is normal. It is human. It is about who is right and who is wrong. It is about who is better. Conflict theorists argue that some problems are to be solved and some are to be managed. I am arguing that interfaith living is a problem to manage, not solve.

According to Speed Leas, a well-known conflict theorist with regard to religious matters in Christian and Jewish settings, the greater the participation of people in the system, the more likely the system is to thrive. The first decision people need to make in a system is whether the conflict is to managed or to be resolved. Better yet that they self-define and negotiate. Then even simple conflict does not get started. The failure to self-define, however, is common enough that conflict is also normal enough.

Leas's theory is summarized in a chart called "Levels of Conflict and Tension in Systems." He specifies five levels. Level 1 is problems to solve, and the goal is to solve the problems. Level 2 is disagreement; the goal is self-protection and coming out looking good. Level 3 is a contest in which the objective is to make sure your position is sustained and your party wins. Level 4 is fight and flight; the objective is to break the relationship either by withdrawing or getting the other to withdraw. Level 5 is the intractable level where the major objective is to destroy the other. Interfaith families have more level 1 than level 5 conflicts — but we remember with everyone what level 5 conflict is, as, for example, in the Holocaust, fueled so well by Jewish-Christian conflict.

Leas offers a theory of polarities that underlies his scale. This scale is useful to the interfaith family because it begins to show how much we might really need each other's difference to become ourselves. In a polarity, both solutions are desired with flexible movements or shifts in emphasis. These are tensions and cannot be solved as problems. One example is how to manage tension between decisiveness and participation. When there is too much decisiveness, we create the need for participation. The opposite is also true. Clarity yields flexibility which reyields the need for clarity. Precision and generality are another example of a polarity, as are rigidity and ambiguity. Law and chaos can dance with grace and order. Management and transformational leadership can take a spin on the floor. These polarities follow the chaos pattern, the yin-yang which is traced in the practice of Tai Chi. In this kind of movement, we function like an oboist, in circular breathing. When we choose to be general, we will create a need to be more precise. Risk reduction calls for risk enhancement, which again calls for risk reduction. We need outreach and inreach. We are "to exhale and inhale but not both at the same time." Leas puts humor to good pedagogical use: a frequently repeated "speedism" is "the answer is yes."

Many of the problems in our family are polarity problems. When we get mad at each other, we accuse in the context of our "battle of the worldviews." The accusations have epithets: "that dumb Jewish legalism of yours" or "that flaky, sappy Resurrection fluff of yours." But what if grace needs law and past needs future? What if hope needs brakes and brakes need hope?

The revived Gesher Theater put on a performance of Joshua Sobol's play *Village*. "What," asks the hero at the end of the play, "is easier to reach, tomorrow or yesterday?" The play, about the fiftieth anniversary of the state of Israel, asks a universal question over which more than one enormous human conflict has erupted.

Not all interfaith families polarize the same ways. I can

imagine a Christian legalist married to a Jewish anarchist. And I don't really see most Judaism and most Christianity as a polarity: they share monotheism and a historical, personal God, as contrasted, for example, with Zen Buddhism. Nevertheless, when conflicts come, we can and do polarize, like most other human beings.

Almost anyone who is asked what makes a good relationship will answer with these words, "I am free to be myself." I don't need the safety of uniformity to be myself. I need to be myself. The other side of the conflict of interfaith life is this joy, this being free to be ourselves. The joy is noticing that we are here and present and visible to another, not distanced, dislocated, or invisible.

Interfaith families are a lot like the Internet. We live in a time when new levels of connection are possible — and thus we make them and enjoy their accompanying conflicts. God is with us — but so also may be the devil. Just because something is new does not mean it is good. Nevertheless, interfaith families encourage people to define themselves by our very presence in a room. When I talk of the goodness and the joy of interfaith living, I am not elevating it to a superior status. Like the jazz movement, it is something that "jes grew." It need not be feared or elevated.

Internet technology has much in common with interfaith families. We "resemble" it — and it resembles us. Because we can connect across cultures, we do. Again, it is important not to overpraise these patterns but to see them with old-fashioned theological eyes. God can use these connections, and God can be abused by these connections.

The Internet has multiplied the possibilities for sin as well as salvation. A student woke his father early one morning. "Dad, wake up. I have to talk to you." They fumbled for coffee and found seats at the kitchen table, and then the sixteen-year-old told his father this story. "I have been having a relationship with a woman on-line. She is a Yale student, she is a beauty queen, she plays varsity tennis. I lied to her. I told her I was a Dartmouth student, a star athlete, a 4.0 student. Now she wants to meet me. What am I going to do?"

The father smiled before he shared his sophisticated theology with his son. "What makes you think that she has been telling the truth about herself?" "Oh, Dad, she would never lie."

The Internet can bring life and it can bring all the problems that human beings bring to life. We can "celebrate diversity" and the cultural police can tell us people that the "new" way is diversity, but the new possibilities for linkage have not eradicated the new possibilities for lying.

In interfaith families there is the heavy historical burden that those who profess Christ might be allowing Christ to disappear historically. Just as Jews worry about dying out, so do Christians worry about being the end of a line of "pure" Christianity.

Virginia Owens asks, "What sign of *Christ* will be left behind when this age is over?"[44] Owens shares the fear that many have of the new possibilities for human linking and blending. In her inability to imagine that some sign of Christ can appear on-line, she encourages the possibility that Christ-like people will resist the new revelation of God.

Owens argues on behalf of the beautiful art of places like Chartres or artifacts like those of Turkey or music like that of Bach and wonders if perhaps the age of the Christian is already over. I doubt it. As wonderful as each of these human creations is, surely new revelations are just as gorgeous. The Holy Spirit can penetrate cyberspace. That penetration is just as easy, or as hard, as building Chartres ever was. Chartres's magnificence or Chagall's paintings did not happen because of the purity of either the Christian moment or the Jewish spirit. They happened because of something larger than either.

The Internet penetrates and permits inner space. Jean Luc Picard on *Star Trek* looked for outer worlds that no one had ever seen before. Captain Kathryn Janeway looked to get "back" home. Both may be on the same journey. I don't see any reason we have to reject a Jewish or Christian history as we embrace a new future. That sounds like making only one choice, for yesterday or tomorrow. The God I know offers both.

Much of this oscillation of past and future polarities and preferences as well as inner and outer space is available because of computers. Men seem to like them even more than women. Men are "discovering" the joy and spaciousness of inner space, which is the place and site of human connection. We are at a moment in history when a larger androgyny might be possible: inner needs outer; history needs nature. Polarities look more ridiculous than ever.

Women have long been more comfortable with getting back to the core, with going inside. I think of Jane Austen's novels or soap operas that spend afternoons talking about what is going on inside homes rather than on the streets and in the offices. I think of the cliché about women always wanting to talk about the relationship and men liking to talk about the route to take to get there. These new valuations of the inner and the relational are points of access to God: we know that creation was a decision to relate to us. We know that Jesus valued Spirit over flesh. We know that the Holy Spirit gets us news of the hope of "things unseen." Computers are helping both men and women access their interiors, while simultaneously sending us to places no one has ever been before.

Nesting and flying are also linked. We are, by the grace of computers and all the other "new" things like air travel and multiculturalism, moving toward a new age of the immediacy of religious experience. Because of these new religious windows and the privacy and safety they offer to so many, we have strong new possibilities for self-focus and self-definition (as well as for delusion, conflict, and reactivity).

We need not know God only by proxy or approved theologies any more. According to Virginia Owens, "The one thing necessary for worship is total presence. Like birth, sex, and death, worship is the only thing left like that. None of these can be performed successfully by proxy or by long distance."[45] Again, I agree with her concern but not her point. Jesus will not be lost but rather found in this new and expanding inner space where people will have a profusion of choices of who their God is.

Given the size of the world's population and its interacting complexity, access to webs and nets is a brilliantly pro-human, pro-communion technology. When we define ourselves in inner space, we look for others who do the same. They don't have to come from our own tribe. We have other options.

"One must enter eternity by time and space. Universality is achieved only by stubborn insistence on locality." So said Chesterton, who continued, "Stay at home, and look deep." Thoreau said that he could see the whole world from Concord if he just looked. Self-definition in a free and linking inner space allows us a religious freedom that is unparalleled in world history. God, in there, is not small at all. God, out there, is not small at all.

Despite her fear of technology, Virginia Owens puts my hope well: "The sustained existence of the church has always been by miracle. . . . Augustine died during the siege of Hippo: things could not have looked good. It will be interesting to see how the Almighty pulls this one off."[46]

I personally yearn for a Jesus-like technology and think that the Internet is very like Jesus. It is user-friendly, it beckons, it invites, it does not require participation, even in goodness. It does not post cultural or denominational police at the gate of the sanctuary. It picks corn on the Sabbath.

We don't need the scientists and technocrats, or Microsoft, to be in charge of culture and art and worship on-line. We need to be in charge ourselves. We need to accept God's offer, from creation on, to create a world in which we can be fully human and fully dedicated to our Creator. "Other" faiths can help us toward full humanity.

The imagery of the Internet as spiral or circle allows for many spiritual points of access. That doesn't mean that it cannot comprehend the linear but rather that it is not limited by it. How do we combine historical religion with spiral religion? Right now, they are in deep conflict; they might yet live in deep polarity.

Cyberspace offers the possibility of wonder and dread for religious people. It fosters a collapse of space, which is scary, particularly for the many peoples of Jerusalem, to which each clings differently. It also ignites fierce economic battles about justice: who can own it? How much money do you need to be able to get on? Are cyberspace and its collapse of space a serious threat to congregational life? Will cyberspace encourage "elective parochiality"? Will we stay at home too much? I can imagine a new Duke Ellington singing, "Don't get around much anymore." Surely, cyberspace transforms what we know of worship and ritual because we can't sing and dance and touch on it. But, I believe, we can pass the peace. We can get around in different ways. We can be totally present on- and off-line. Interfaith people are not the only ones making this journey to a religion beyond the space of our holy historical city, Jerusalem. The aesthetic and religious imaginations have always risen to material challenges before. We can rise and reweb and restore (*tikkun olam*) again.

New economies call out new conflicting worldviews and bring forth new revelations from God. "The fact is there is very little economic room in the physical world these days. If you are making something you can touch, and doing well at it, then you are either an Asian or a machine."[47]

Kevin Kelley, executive editor of *Wired* magazine, says,

> My advice would be to open your mind to the possibility that in creating Cyberspace we've made a new space for literature and art, that we have artists working there who are as great as artists in the past. They're working in a medium that you might dismiss right now as inconsequential, just as the theater, in Shakespeare's day, was dismissed as outrageous and low class and not very deep.[48]

Our space is threatened and so is our narrative thread. Jews and Christians actually have a common battle with the spiral. We are very historical believers. But Janet Horowitz Murray makes the point that narrative is comprehended in a larger and still threatened circularity.[49] What will address these threats to our several historical, space-bound faiths is not a fight between us but a conversation with the future. That conversation will be fundamentally spiritual. It will borrow from deep patterns in our faiths.

Chapter Eight

Monotony, Monotheism, and Maturity

Interfaith people do not cease to be monotheists: instead, we worship one God of many and diverse expressions, fully aware that our God is not the only face of the one true God. Our faith matures into something humble toward God.

William James, the author of the seminal work *The Varieties of Religious Experience,* says that he is much more interested in the varieties of religious experience than he is in the unities. So am I. I know too many different kinds of people to imagine only one God. The one God I know enjoys being many. The old joke about Jews (two Jews, three opinions) is also frequently circulated in United Church of Christ circles, where the version is "two Congregationalists, three opinions." All by my unitary self I may enjoy three opinions on one matter. I don't think I am strange. I am single and I am variety.

James makes a theological method out of focusing on the particular as opposed to the universal. His own view of evil is that it is the totalizing impulse, in which the unity proper only to the one God takes the place that particularity should rightly have.

Here I am going to argue for monotheism with a small *m*, an open monotheism. Not absolute. I am going to argue for monotheism, not Monotheism. There is a difference. One is beautiful and makes space for beauty. The other is ugly and shuts things down. It is a cage, and no one dare cage God.

James helps us see the aesthetic injury, in addition to the political and social injury of Monotheism. Monotony is the political, social, and aesthetic injury of Monotheism. A smaller word could be used: Monotheism is dull. In a description of the difference between Protestants and Catholics James says,

> Although Protestants aim at intellectual purity and sim-
> plification, for others richness is the supreme imagi-
> nation requirement. . . . How flat does evangelical Prot-
> estantism appear, how bare the atmosphere of those
> isolated religious lives whose boast it is that man in the
> bush with "God" may meet. What a pulverization and
> leveling of what a gloriously piled up structure. . . . To
> an imagination used to the perspectives of dignity and
> glory, the naked gospel scheme seems to offer an alms-
> house for a palace. When one gives up the titles of
> dignity, the crimson lights and blare of brass, the gold
> embroidery, the plumed troops, the fear and trembling
> [of Roman Catholicism] and puts up with a president in
> a black coat who shakes hands with you, and comes, it
> may be, from a home and puts the bible on a center
> table, it pauperizes the monarchical imagination. The
> strength of these aesthetic sentiments makes it rigor-
> ously impossible that Protestantism, however superior
> in spiritual profundity it may be to Catholicism, should

at the present succeed in making many converts from
the more venerable ecclesiasticism. The latter offers a
so much richer pasturage and shade to the fancy, and
so many cells with so many different kinds of honey,
is so indulgent in its multiform appeals to human nature, that Protestantism will always show to Catholic
eyes the almshouse physiognomy. The bitter negativity
of it is to the Catholic mind incomprehensible. . . . To the
Catholic the Protestant appears as morose as if he were
some hard eyed numb monotonous kind of reptile. The
two will never understand each other, their centers of
emotional energy are too different.[50]

Monotheism undergirds the monotony of which James
speaks. It makes us choose between the wealth of one pattern
and the completely different wealth of another. Never mind
that we are comparing Catholics and Protestants; Jews and
Christians keep as much distance as these two. Monotheism
sets up false choices. It "punyizes" God, as my son Isaac
said of a boy who hit another boy with a stick. Isaac said
that the boy who hit had punyized himself. I like his word
better than "belittle." James's embroidered prose echoes the
words of a six-year-old to describe how horrifying it is when
we make our God small. When we cage our God, we abuse
monotheism.

Others would argue for color and variety in a different
way. They would hate the plumes with vigor. They would
point to Catholic distaste for women and for gays and ridicule the vaunted "richness" in that position. But lovers of
difference understand that we have rights to conflict. To be a
lover of difference is to enjoy the tension in the rival claims.
It is not to try to get to the worship of the right God. It is to
worship our god, not God.

Bernie Glassman, a former Jew and now Zen master, advocates a "house of one people" with many rooms. He argues for a space not only where people of different religions dialogue or hold joint celebrations, but also where all of us, while upholding our separate paths, will be one people.[51] I understand his desire for one house; it is a deep and vivid spiritual impulse. I simply want that house to have many rooms and to have them interconnected, the way I imagine God as a universe with doors and windows. My faith is in a God who loves my room and your room, not either but both.

Faith is a new way of seeing. If anything, religious experience drives us to unity in a way that nothing else does. It binds. It coheres. It knits and threads and tries to make fragments whole. That unifying impulse is the central religious impulse; if I am made by God and you are made by God, then maybe we even have something in common. Having something in common does not mean that we are the same. We can have in common the fact that we are different.

Everyone knows Dorothy, that little girl that left gray, one-dimensional Kansas to move into the multicolor, multilevel world of Oz. Dorothy, a naif who got thoroughly confused about home and thought that home was safety, nevertheless uprooted herself, or had herself uprooted. Dorothy sings a hymn to elsewhere, but it is an elsewhere that cannot be reached.

Is a religious faith that is "elsewhere" and "can't be reached" legitimate? Or realistic? My heart thinks so. My eyes think so. Others don't always agree. I can just hear my college dean now. I always thought of him as the reality police. He thought my ideas about faith as a new way of seeing were not "realistic." That is to say, they can't be put into practice by the current administration. That's right. But that's because these ideas imagine a new administration.

College by college. One less capable of hanging on and more capable of letting go. The deans are right because the new way of seeing has to precede — not follow — the educational strategies.

Faith is a unifying way of seeing that comprehends diversity — the comprehension of which itself is unifying. First, we jump and then we get our wings, to repeat Ray Bradbury. With Walter Brueggemann, I like to live as the gospel were true, not as if. In *Texts under Negotiation*, Brueggemann suggests leaving out the "if" because saying it turns faith into something unreal.[52]

To me saying "be realistic" is just another way of saying "we like it the way it is." It is not just a childlike faith that demands that I propose implausibility and unreality for a spiritual basis but the political fact that I don't like it the way it is. Neither do most women, the poor, the lame, the sick, the old, or the two-thirds world. Those who like the way it is are a very small minority who have not only claimed most of the money and most of the deanships but also most of the interpretive world. Brueggemann declares an emergency in interpretation, and it is a tremendous relief to see a white man do so. Most people live in that emergency most of the time. Monotheism is an idea from the old regime. We who know we live in an interpretative emergency are not as fond of monotheism as we might be. We don't want to be caged and we don't want our God caged.

I not only dislike the way things are spiritually and politically but also aesthetically. Things this way are monotonous. They are monocultural. They are dull. Thus my allegiance to Dorothy. I am both afraid to be like her and afraid not to be like her, which is to say that fear accompanies travel. And that it is fear that makes travel an adventure. In the monotonous worlds from which most of us think we come — in fact they are as colorful as Oz — we are usually so safe that we are dead. Or at least dying from boredom. Monocultures are monotonous; multicultures are interesting.

The adventure beyond dullness is hermeneutical first. "Hermeneutic" is a big word denoting how we see what we see and whether we can see more ways than just the way our culture sees. This point goes for first- and third-world cultures as well as for colleges who think only Ph.D.'s can teach or that "unrealistic" things are dangerous. We are all endangered, blocked, and prejudiced at the level of eyesight.

Difference is dangerous. Any kind of difference. Had I shown up at work today not wearing the right kind of clothes, I would experience a modest form of the danger. At this first level it is simply embarrassment. But at the deeper and more systemic levels the danger is violence. It is Croats and Moslems, Jews and Arabs, men and women, rich and poor. Fear of difference is the root cause of the thermonuclear war we may yet have. Fear of difference is the root of racism and sexism. When all we can do is fear difference, we suffer monotony and we create a situation in which we have to arm ourselves against difference rather than learn to appreciate it.

Monotony is the first station on the road to violence. It is also the cause of our joylessness. Oz has color. Kansas is gray. Our destination is a colorful Kansas, a real place where difference is really enjoyed.

I see the monotony in all the restaurant jelly packets that are the same square shape, that open the same way, that are cherry or strawberry or the occasional marmalade. I see it in the ubiquitous BIC pen. I see it in housing segregation so serious that Rodney King couldn't go to a suburb and find a jury of his peers, thereby shaking the very foundation of our judicial system. I see it in people who wouldn't think of staying in any other motel than a Howard Johnson's. The refusal of the adventure of difference has made American culture boring. Our fear of difference, which includes but is not limited to our racism, has turned what could yet be a vibrant culture into a strip mall. Bored to death we might say. Not the kind of death that calls the undertaker but rather the wages-of-sin kind.

Monotheism is at the bottom of the boredom. Multiculturalism and diversity are the route out of the trouble. The route is both an aesthetic and a social adventure. I think of chokecherry jelly or beach plum jam and I get excited. I take a little trip to Oz. I meet something that is a stranger to me. I like it. In the same terms, those of gladness, those of gratitude, I think of God's project in history being completed, of all the power in creation being fully distributed, of beautiful housing for everyone. Racism, thus seen, is boring. It is monotonous. It is not the intention of creation to be gray. Racism is an aesthetic offense as much as it is a social offense. Racism is the victory of Kansas over Oz, the victory of gray over color, the victory of fear over grace. (By the way, I am delighted to thank Salman Rushdie, the Moslem who had to hide because of his threat to Iranian Monotheism, for many of these ideas about the Wizard of Oz.) The Kansas monotony is the simple form of racism.

In Numbers 15 we are told that the stranger is to have all the rights of community while he or she is in the community. I think of this as a tribal advance. The tribes were experimenting with a little multicultural justice. Civilization has now moved beyond the need for tribal regulation; most of our rights travel with us. Our souls may not have moved much beyond fear of the strange; our theologies may not have kept pace. But the world has changed. Now the question is much more about how the different tribes can enjoy the stranger's gifts, not about how the stranger can be safe in our tribe (although there are many neighborhoods where you better be the right color to be safe). The question is how we can enjoy what the stranger brings to our monoculture.

Jesus took this justice toward the stranger in a myriad of ways. He showed how the strangers were outsiders, and he brought the outsiders in. I think of the Kingdom parables in particular, what we now call the stories of the new realm: the prodigal son, the lost sheep, the lost coin, the workers in the vineyard, the weeds, the net, the growing seed, the talents, the yeast, the wedding banquet, the ten coins, the persistent widow, the rich man and Lazarus, the sheep and goats, the tenants, the wise and foolish builders. It is hard to think of a parable where a dull inside circle is not livened up by an outsider's entrance, brokered by Jesus Christ. The monotony is broken, the stranger is welcomed, and the new realm is the transformation of the old realm from a dead and dull place into a new and lively one. Brueggemann describes this change as the move from settled reality to storied reality, that place where God's fiction is more powerful than the world's fact. Sounds a lot like Oz to me.

I am taking the injury of boredom as equal to the injury of injustice. Or rather, I am taking a decidedly white point of view on racism. I am talking about how it hurts me. Do I think that racism has hurt me anywhere near as much as it has hurt people who are not white? No. That would be like complaining that one's front row seat is uncomfortable while other people are sitting on the floor. The matter of scale is not being addressed here. The matter of shape is. Racism is at least the fear of difference. Racism is the refusal of the theological adventure of worlds of color. Racism is clinging to Kansas so hard that we are condemned to stay there. When people of color develop attitudes about white people that refuse their difference, the same theological adventure is refused. That refusal is an insult to creation, an aesthetic sin as much as it is a social sin. The emergency in interpretation underlies the problem that is expressed here as social injustice. If God is one, and my God is best, everybody else better watch out. I may have to destroy you for my God.

It is bad enough that the majority of Americans seem to want their culture to be predictable and stagnant and monotonous. It is worse that we allow fewer and fewer people to control the economy, thus compounding the racial fear of difference into an economic tyranny. The right to control the market is directly related to racism, which is the progeny of Monotheism. If you believe that you have a right to control your boundaries against the invasion of other tribes, then you not only refuse the gifts of the stranger; you also build fences so high the stranger can't get in. Most of us know this better in our personal relationships than in our public relationships; we know how much controlling our borders hurts us and how much disarmament can help us.

At this stage in the development of the American economy, it is very hard for the people who are "out" to get in. The fences are too high. Although the mythology of the open market is very much alive, in fact, even if you make the best jelly in the world, you're going to have a hard time breaking into the breakfast market. Working harder or better will not get you in. The monotonists will keep you out.

Monotheism births monotony. Monotony damages beauty and causes injustice. Fear of difference is at the basis of the monotony. Were we able to maturely love difference and conquer our fear of it, we could enjoy more beautiful worlds. And jellies. And just communities. Some people's children would not be eating the lead paint of other people's myths. Were we able to worship the unified God who chooses diversity, even in the very self of God, we could move beyond these fears. We could be less bored. And less dangerous.

Kansas and Oz, color and gray, simple and complex. It is, Rushdie reminds us, the grayness of the tornado unleashed upon itself that is the problem. It is the way Kansas thinks it is everything that is the problem, not Kansas itself. It is the way Kansas thinks that its god is everything, not its God, that is the problem.

So what can we do about monotony and its double crimes, its crimes against beauty and its crimes against justice? From the point of view of my community, which is the United Church of Christ, we can always be careful about our voice, our tone, acknowledging that it is mono-tonous. Monotony is not just an individual voice but rather a culture voice that has become imperial. The United Church of Christ carries just enough of the American baggage that we house imperialism that we haven't even unpacked yet. We should use our voice and praise our God — vigorously. If anything we should become more ourselves over time. (The Dalai Lama always tells people who want to become Buddhist to go home, back to Kansas, and become who you are.) But we need not make everyone else over into our own image. Our voice is just that, wonderfully, our voice. It does not speak for everyone.

Leaving the old Kansas can be very painful. It can mean killing off some parts of the old gods, and even some parts of our parents. We have to make room for good tether; we have to release ourselves from bad tether. This process of choice involves a loosening of the knot, not an untying or breaking out of it. It involves getting to know the pieces of the braid. It means making friends with the tether, not untethering. We'll probably never be free of the obnoxious God, or parent, but we can at least see the knot and let our skin heal from the damage it has done. Scars will remain. Knots are nests. The spiritual work/play of untethering from the old Monotheist on behalf of the God who loves us all is best done in a nest, piece by piece, string by string, twig by twig. Learning to love diversity is slow work but it does lead to God.

God, Alpha, Omega, beginning, end. With a ball of yarn, all you have to do is find one end. Then you can go muddle along toward order. We are assured of a pattern in eternity, that God is the start and the finish line, the Creator and the Redeemer — *in whom* we live and move and have our being. I like the "in" part. The obvious truth is that, if God is alpha and omega, God has a middle also. I just never expected to find so much God in so many places. How else could God be one and everywhere at the same time?

I remember the "stranger God" in the Easter hymns I sang as Jacob's respirator was removed at age fourteen days. I was in a crowded hospital room with Jacob and twenty-nine tubes — and forty other preemies struggling for breath. My, how God gets around. When Jacob's respirator came off, the woman next to me asked if I would sing for her child. I did. It was then that my tears finally flowed.

The Zen patriarch and Chinese sage Hui Neng says that the meaning of life is to see. Who cares if we see the right God? Or the one true God? Who really cares? As long as we see God. As long as we are accompanied and get a glimpse and are sure that God is fair and that God is with the other preemies as well as with our Jacob.

When I quarrel with Monotheism, I am not suggesting an "individual" or "personal" God. That God would also be too small, just in another way. T. S. Eliot must have felt this when he wrote, "Art is not to express personality, but to overcome it." When I talk about seeing, I talk about getting enough of myself out of the way so that the strings, in all their separate beauty, can be seen for what they are. Even knotted.

Frederick Franck speaks of the way self-centeredness knots us even tighter.[53] He recalls a formative life experience of listening to some music in a park as a child when he first "disappeared." All became one. He transcended himself. Some of my best pastors become "invisible" in their systems. I don't know quite how to do that but every now and then it happens. Sometimes I loosen the knots that tie me and protect me and hold me so that something of use can happen with my life. I want to get out of my own way. I want to see God. I want to walk with God. Again, not the one true God, but just God.

Franck also talks about the great music of Bach in a way that demonstrates the method here. He says that Bach was not expressing himself so much as letting the sacred express itself through him. Art, says Franck, is that which, despite all, gives hope.

When we disappear and get out of our way and loosen and appreciate the cords that bind us, the sacred has a chance with us. When we do not, the sacred is as shut out of our lives as we are. Beyond Monotheism, I want to look through the gaps in the yarn. The little openings. The unexpected lights in the tunnels of connection and reconnection. I want to see God. The way God has seen — and watched over — me. The strategy: Look. See. Don't expect to see monotheism, or monotony, or anything. Just look and see. I see the sufficiency of tethered sight, the sources of which are at least two ancient and venerable faith traditions plus a little more.

I learned the most about monotony and monotheism and faith the day I found myself telling my therapist that "Tinker Bell died." She couldn't fly any more. She had to learn how to live on the ground. I was in a grown-up battle between faith and doubt. I had to refocus my faith. It couldn't just be in my many abilities but rather had to be in something beyond and under my abilities.

My most often recurring dream has been one that involved transmuting gossamers. In the positive, comforting dream, all my projects and children and friends are attached to me by great gossamer strings. They are crocheted and beautiful, and my companions and I fly about. When I get tired, as I now do more frequently much to my personal embarrassment, the gossamer turns to chains. To move, I have to pick up each burden individually and toss it ahead of me, the way heavily burdened passengers move their luggage, one piece at a time. The dream can keep me "busy" all night, changing the gossamer to iron and back. I lose projects and people along the way, like so many lost socks in the mess of the kids' rooms. When my father died, the angels told me in the middle of one long night: "You are too heavy. We are going to have to add gossamer. Give us some time." The "one true God" does not help so much at moments like this as does God. Just God.

Monotheism could never have managed this or any of the other dozen faith crises I have had over time. Spiritual development is this nearly constant changing, beyond monotony and monotheism. New Gods come to us over time. They ask us to give them some time.

I know a seventy-year-old woman who fell in love, "extra-curricularly." I know an octogenarian who is begging his son to let him ride his motorcycle. I also know some adolescents who show astonishing maturity. Maturity is not a progression. It is a new relationship to our ties and tethers. A knot grows tighter if you work against it; it grows looser as you let it be and follow its own irregularity. What little I know of

God is plenty to last a lifetime. "The smaller I make them, the bigger they get," said the Italian sculptor Giacometti, commenting on his work. So it has been with me and God. God is very small and particular to me now. And larger than ever before.

"Parochialism has become untenable.... Today we know that even the solar system is not the center of the universe," says Heschel. He understood how in the true God, not the "one true God," anti-Semitism is anti-Christianity and vice versa.[54] He understood that the most important prerequisite for people who live in interfaith relationships is faith. "Holiness is not the monopoly of any particular religion or tradition. Whenever a deed is done in accord with the will of God, whenever human thought is directed toward Him, there is the holy."[55] Unlike William James, Heschel testifies to the diversity by pointing to the unity. No one direction is complete. Not even people as great as James or Heschel can be counted on to get it "right."

One of the most moving treatments of God for me is Korean theologian Chun Hyun-Kyung's address to the Canberra Assembly of the World Council of Churches. She invokes the Spirit through the spirits of all the oppressed, from the murdered "spirit of the Amazon rain forest," to victims of the Holocaust and Hiroshima, as well as Hagar, Jephthah's daughter, Malcolm X, Oscar Romero, and all other life forms, human and nonhuman, that "like the Liberator, our brother Jesus," have been tortured and killed for greed and in hate. In this stunning hymn to the spirit, she invokes a God who is one and many:

Dear Brothers and Sisters, with the energy of the Holy Spirit let us tear apart all walls of division and the culture of death which separate us. And let us participate

in the Holy Spirit's political economy of life, fighting for
our life on this earth in solidarity with all living beings
and building communities for justice, peace, and the integrity of creation. Let us welcome her, letting ourselves
go in her wild rhythm of life. Come Holy Spirit, renew
the whole creation.

The only problem I have with her prayer is that it slips
into a totalizing impulse itself. Why the whole creation? Why
not one piece at a time, where the oppressed participate in
their own renewal, twig by twig? Why should the World
Council of Churches bother with the new movements of
transnational engaged Buddhism or Japanese Shintos? Why
not pray for each other and hope for each other in a mature
faithful path of seeing each other well enough that we see all
the way to a monotheistic God, who belongs to each but to
none all by themselves? Chun Hyun-Kyung, as wise as she is,
cannot be counted on to get it right all by herself either.

Mature faith is monotheistic, not Monotheistic. It is multicultural in a genuine way, not monocultural. God really does
love us all.

Chapter Nine

A Letter to My Grandchildren

I find it audacious even to address you because my experience is so contrary to what I thought it would be. I was born a Missouri Synod Lutheran, worshiped in German, was rigidly taught my catechism — and was assured that Catholics were not only wrong about God, but wrong in an evil way. I was taught they were going to hell for being different and "not as good" as us. Then, after being ordained in the United Church of Christ, I married a Jew.

If I could not have known what was coming, neither can you. I never expected to marry a Jew, or to raise children "both ways." I was and am a Christian. But Christianity has expanded as a home for me. You may start out Jewish. Or Buddhist. You will start with at least one parent who was raised both Jewish and Christian: God only knows who the other one will be. Or whether your second set of genes will come from a test tube.

One of your great aunts on my side is half Korean; next year I hope to attend her wedding to a French cook. I hope you will enjoy your second cousins. Stranger things have happened. I probably won't know you since I gave birth to your parent when I was thirty-eight. If the trend toward older mothers continues, you will arrive after I am gone. By then this Korean-French family will be sending their children to college. Maybe in Mozambique. You may not even know them, but I wanted you to know about them.

I had four living grandparents when I arrived. From them I learned a lot about fundamentalist Christianity. From me you will get something different.

Feminism exploded my world as much as Judaism did: it invited me to become both a mother and a minister. And I accepted the invitation. Feminism assured me that I could do both. You will therefore get to tell your children that "my grandmother was a sort of pioneer as an ordained woman minister."

They may find that very strange since, by then, women will be everywhere in all the professions. I am sitting right now next to the *New Yorker* magazine for May 1998. On the cover is a picture entitled, "Lunch Break." A female construction worker in a hard hat is nursing a baby. Again, that seems strange to me and delightfully comic. To you it will probably seem ordinary.

I must tell you a story about my firstborn, Isaac. He accompanied me to a clergy breakfast meeting once when he was five. All the other clergy there were men. He was upset: "Mommy, boys can't be ministers." Big changes have happened in my life. Surely, they will happen in yours as well. Stay away from the words "can't" and "never"; go with the words "might yet be" and "possible." These are religious words: God likes them.

You will be like me — and not just because change will mark your life. You will also likely be someone who runs between the particular and the general, the forest and the trees. You'll want to own your origin, your story, your tribe — and you'll want like hell to get away from it and be uniquely composed.

I have gone from one who filled in the religious preference question on college applications with "nothing" to exploding the line of personal explanation. I am a Christian who loves Judaism — and often refer to myself as "Zenny." I do Tai Chi and yoga every day. I garden for and to God. Nature joins history and body joins mind in praising God. I am more than a little bit pagan.

The writer Jim Heynen said that his inherited faith was a noose that kept him from hanging. I like that kind of religious "koan," or conundrum: life has been like that for me. Love is something that kept me from falling: I loved your parent to hold myself up. I received more than I gave. I gave to get. I am not ashamed of this paradox because it reminds me of the golden rule, which both Jews and Christians enjoy: "Do unto others as you would have them do unto you," or, "Don't do anything you wouldn't want done to you." I love to be loved; I give up my life to get it. You'll understand these things after they happen to you; that's how faith works.

My hope for you is that you will know God — because God is more magnificent than anything or anyone else. And that says a lot because so many things are so magnificent. I hope you will have been taught the golden rule so that when your life teaches it to you, which it will, you will have the memory of our people ringing in your ears. First as an echo, and then a claim, something you will also tell your children.

When it comes to the trees in the forest, it is very important to be something — not everything. Such grounding will be very hard for you because you will have at least two homes. So go to them both and live them! Give up everything to which you do not belong — and know that you belong to a lot. Live from a mansion, not a tree house! Human beings don't only go forward to home; we also go backward to home. And Christianity is nested in Judaism.

I hope you will live antagonistically toward the general and lovingly toward the particularities of your two faiths of origin. I am afraid of relativism. First General Foods, then General Motors, now General Devotional! The juice and the joy are removed from franchised spirituality. Scripture is used generically; inspiration is offered at the lowest possible common denominator. Feel-goodism has found a new proponent; the Sheilas of the world will love it. ("Sheila," described by social scientist Robert Bellah, worships herself.) In General Faith, sin is clearly a fantasy of the theological past. If something goes wrong, or might go wrong, or did go wrong, it's the fault of improper daily schedules or inputs.

These theological and spiritual problems are generated from division by the lowest possible American denominator, a de-ethnicizing of religion, and a monotonous brush-off of genuine religious culture. Here, we get "inner peace promoting healing of mind and body," a kind of fast-food chicken nugget meal, tasting way too much like chicken soup for the soul. "If I am feeling under the weather, I can nourish my immune system with prayer." I take a "serenity break." Such approaches can be valid, but their truths are hidden in too large a frame. Artists know: to make one thing larger in a picture, sometimes other things have to become smaller.

Kathleen Norris said what I feel about life in and around my beautiful tree in one corner of the forest or airport or world. "I often think that if I am a Christian, I'll be the last to know."[56] I believe in a Jesus Christ who would never insist on imperialism, even regarding the one he called Father. I hold my Christ in an open hand.

You'll probably want to know what I think about the Trinity if you get into Christianity very far. It is the three-in-one God who allows Christians often to be such a pain to Jews. We try to incorporate their God into ours, which is not very fair. We try to put them in our nest — when we live in theirs.

The main way I have faced differences the size of these is to define myself without trying to control others. The capacity to act without controlling is the way of Tai Chi: I try to follow that way. I am going to tell you how I feel about Jesus as a way of making sure you know the source of my security and safety and salvation. Not as a way of arguing for Christianity against Judaism — or the superiority of grandmothers over grandfathers. Mingle your roots and enjoy them.

I believe in the Trinity because it pleases me so as an explanation of the majesty and fluidity of God. I don't believe in it absolutely. I feel I might be wrong as well as right.

I have to admit that I don't really understand the Jews or the Unitarians or other so-called universalists from my spot in the forest. Why leave the interesting parts of God's self-disclosure? Why let go of the blood of Jesus, the decision of God to mix up with humanity? If we are blended people, then why would God not be a blend of heaven and earth, body and soul, divine and human as well?

One of the ways I am a tree — and not a forest — is that I believe in Jesus Christ as my Lord and Savior. Some of the people I love the most in the world don't! I don't understand why, but I do understand *that* they see Jesus as much less than I see Jesus.

I do not find the way many Jews substitute Israel, the land, for Christ very appealing. It seems to me to be idolatrous because a nation is not a God. Not to mention the hurt that has come to the Palestinians and the Christians in Jerusalem. The God I know doesn't favor one tribe over another. But I have learned that people do think this way and that I need to be very cautious about calling other people idolatrous.

I don't know what will have become of Israel by the

time you are born. I do know that for a long time Christians couldn't even talk about Israel without getting in trouble. The reasons are multiple: they include the history of Christianity's treatment of Jews and the horrors of the Second World War. You will know about the Holocaust by now. I hope you also know a story of human goodness of similar size.

My problem as a Christian was not just that I fell in love with your grandfather — and was born with a love of the "edge." It is also that I never could imagine being monotheist when there are so many sites and experiences of the sacred — but that is more a personality problem in me, the Gemini, than it is a theological comment. I like lots of everything — so the more Gods and types of Gods the better. I understand others find that offensive to God — and swear at me with words like "pantheist." Which is unfair — because there are a few things that don't remind me of God. And ask them to look up the much more suitable word "panentheist": it is a better word for me.

I simply love the idea of God becoming human. It strikes me as just the kind of thing God would do. The incarnation of God in flesh, in Jesus, gets very difficult for people, especially Jews and Unitarians. It is this very coming and going — this flow, this interior, this passage through and in time — that enamors me about the Trinity. I like the fleeting sense of the Trinitarian God. I like particular things. And bodily things. And meaty things. And because I have an enormous, avaricious sense of abundance, the fact that things, even things godly, pass doesn't really bother me. More God is on the way when some God passes. The Holy Spirit actually permeates the universe as far as I am concerned.

Theologians like Karl Barth argue that our language about God should begin with language about Christ. I used to think that before I married your grandfather. I loved Christ so much, intellectually and experientially, that I had no need for a faraway God. Now I pray to the faraway God as a matter of respect for others.

From Hispanics and from liberation theology, I have learned that the incarnation exemplifies the ultimate *mestizaje,* the juncture of divinity and humanity. Their liberation theologies have meant a lot to me. For people so oppressed to know God so well is another of the many paradoxes that please me. I love the fact that people who are probably as different from me as I am from your grandfather have a sense of what I feel about the Trinity. This connection with another tree in the forest matters a lot to me.

Both the Germans of my origin and the American Hispanics argue for Christ in a way that the Universalist types do not. Their historical experience made them want a larger, further away God; others wanted a God closer up. God has never been far from me, not even for a day. I dip deep and there God is, in my heart. I have direct religious experience all the time — and am stunned to discover that many others do not.

I want you to feel God. If you can't pray or if prayer doesn't come easy to you, simple sway, or daven, or bow, or get on your knees every now and then. Jews have always "danced" toward God when words didn't work. What is significant is the piety, the decision for a piety, the memory of the piety and the music and the dance. These stay with us long after hope is gone. Yes, hope does flee, even for people full of faith. It returns also: we have pain and hope and often don't know the real source of either. Melody has often carried hope for me when my mind and heart had quit.

Let me tell you what happened on the day of the twenty-fifth anniversary of my ordination to the ministry. It will show you the way God talks to me. My maker offered me another twenty-five years! The offer was direct and personal. She (I call God "she" even though I know she is more than any gender) often speaks quite directly to me. I refer to God as "my maker" in the privacy of my own self. Actually, God is my best friend. But in public, I almost always pray to the other name of my close friend — to "the God beyond God, the God whom some call Allah, and some call Jesus, and some call Yahweh or Adonai, the God beyond all names."

According to Orlando Costas, one of my favorite theologians, the incarnation forces us to contextualize God's activity within history, preventing us from turning God into an abstract being removed from human experience. My God is very close — but I have learned that God is also big.

Each road has a different vice and a different virtue. We, for example, are scared to death that our children will pick "his" or "her" faith when they mature. The idea that my children could become Jewish, by conversion, when I am a Christian minister didn't both me at all at first. I figured my side would win out. As your grandfather became more observant as the children grew older — a normal enough pattern — the children identified more and more with his faith. It terrified me. I don't like it. But I am learning to live with the God beyond God — who has put me through more than this on behalf of the Holy.

Parents who are not from different faith origins have no insurance policy on their children's future either, so I own the sneaky tribalism of my fear. You may even decide to marry somebody just like you, a blended faith. Why not? That is up to you. God can be many and one; God can be beyond God and beyond any denominational, or parochial, or ethnic, or national knowing. God can be *Unum* as well as *Pluribus*.

Some say each partner in a marriage should give 50 percent. I believe each partner should give 100 percent, and even then they may not have a complete covenant. When I speak of the many different authentic revelations, I am talking about this kind of math. Even with all our faiths, in full traditional regalia, we probably still don't know all there is to know about God. Interfaith families believe in the largeness of God.

The new deck on the back of our house may be another way to understand this notion of the size of God. The deck itself is inconsequential — but what it represents is not. A heavy snow on April 1 last year, the day after Easter, knocked down the old arbor, built on the base of the old barn, which held up the old deck. Crash. The insurance people said we were able to collect only $3000 to undertake what was clearly a $6000 project. For months, we rung our hands. What to do? We looked all spring at the mess of ancient wisteria wound around rotted poles, yellow rose bushes unable to make their annual climb. All of a sudden the idea came: the new deck could easily be half the size of the old deck. Also half the price. Our trusty contractor agreed and designed a new deck that snuggles up to the back of the house as though it was part of the original design. People stop to ask who built it, so nicely does it fit. And we have a morality play in our back yard: downsizing, designed well, may be the best thing to do on many fronts.

When we become smaller, we rightsize. But we dare not downsize or even rightsize our God. We need to be careful not to let God get caught in the net. A revelation that founds a particular faith may be full; it may be authentic. But it is not complete. God is larger than any one faith. We need to know our right size — but our right size is not God's size.

Too many religious faiths act like discount airlines: they offer the cheapest, safest flight possible. They turn their specialness into the lowest common denominator to make it palatable. They lose the power of the "small" right-sized traditions in order to blend. Instead, we might accentuate the peculiarities of our faith and rightsize them. Everyone doesn't have to light candles on Friday. Everyone doesn't have to sing the Gloria on Sunday. But some people do and will: they don't do it out of imperialism but rather out of a redesign of their conception of their religious deck, the deck that marries their house and "fits" onto it. When we let God be big, other things can be appropriately small.

When we don't go to your great grandparents' home, we often celebrate Easter with another interfaith family with kids the same age as ours. They are raising their children different than we are. We are raising ours "both ways" — not because we think we are right but because we believe that God has given us permission to pioneer. They are raising theirs one way. He is Jewish; she is a Christian minister. At Easter, we have a little Seder. Once we ate a ham. We're not the only people pushing these kinds of envelopes.

As Richard Carlson puts it, Don't sweat the small stuff, and, by the way, it's all small stuff. Treasure the small. Treasure the little. Treasure! That's what the God beyond God, the God of Passover and Easter wants. What we treasure is our particularity in the large forest. We treasure our nest within the nest.

I have found my way to God through the ancient wisdom of my tree, the golden rule theology. I have found my way to God through the Trinity. I have found my way to God by "going home" and living from one spot. I have also found my way to God through "art" for lack of a better word. "Poetry is not a luxury," said Adrienne Rich, one of my favorite poets.

In *Letters and Papers from Prison* Dietrich Bonhoeffer

spoke of communities of faith in modernity cultivating the "arcane disciplines" of prayer, meditation, and worship. Each of these is poetry to me; there is nothing I would rather do than pray or sing or worship. These things mark me. They are the words I know by heart, the melodies that I sing when I have to go through something hard, like getting a tooth drilled or birthing a baby or holding my temper.

I hope you also will know a regular piety, a way like the one our family used for the Friday candles of simple blessing, continuous repetition of song, words that became so familiar we have to use them when something bad happens so we can cry and mourn and grieve. I hope your faith will be ordinary and close to you. I hope your faith will assist you in not becoming cold. Memorized prayers and songs are crucial. I hope you will know some.

This brings me to another way I have known God — one that I strongly recommend. I have known God in trying to understand why evil exists, why some people remain poor, why people shoot each other. In her poem "Blazes," Penelope Duckworth speaks of a fireplace as "bounded evil, managed fire." I suffer because others suffer. I have suffered myself. When I suffer, I use rituals, poetry, music, worship to put salve on my wounds. I manage the evil with a religious tradition.

I have traveled the world and the cities of America, and I have seen and known lots of poverty. I started out poor myself, but then I got rich. I met a girl on the Croatian border who had nothing but stale green bread in her pocket. She was a refugee at age eleven. I pray for her every day because otherwise she would break my heart.

You should know a little of what I do for a living. I help churches stay well as institutions. The reason I do this kind of work is that I believe the gospel of Jesus Christ, well tended by strong institutions, is the best contribution I can make to the girls with green bread in their pocket. As an area minister in the UCC, I go out to visit the churches in my area. Often the first question the committee asks me is, "What are you doing here?" I usually mumble something, like I was invited. Ten minutes later, the background of the question surfaces: "And where were you, representing the wider church, when such and such happened?" Do you see the double bind? Come closer, get away. Get away, come closer. Leave us alone, but don't neglect us.

We all want lots of freedom and lots of community. We rarely can have both, but this is what we want and this is what God wants for us. I see my ministry as partnership with God in God's plan to bring the world into full covenant with our Maker. God's purpose in history is to redistribute power so that all people have a full life — which is fully autonomous and fully connected. We are to be able to be fully, uniquely ourselves, our own tree, and fully and completely connected to each other. I do a little bit institutionally every day to make that world happen for me and for others. I believe in the vessels that hold faith and do not join most Americans today in their distrust of institutions. I think people need them, and I believe that the ancient paths, rightly contained and bounded, can be vessels of God.

We are witnessing today nothing less than a renewed battle between the new gods and the old gods. Just as in the Reformation God showed more of God's self as the economy and political structure changed, so it is again today. And we are here, we are now, we can see and hear it. It is a profound blessing to live in such interesting times.

If I have any religious advice for you at all, it is to say watch out for the polarizers, those who try to separate religion and politics, or body and soul, or heaven and earth.

Watch the struggle between bread and freedom: you not only can have both but you must have both.

Many will take freedom and forget community — or take bread and forget joy. They are accepting cheap gifts, the kind Dostoyevsky's Grand Inquisitor gave. By cheating people out of their humanity and offering them security instead, like many of our churches do, we offer each other a life of incoherence. For me, Christ brings the people to scary freedom and good bread, not the cheap bread of traded freedom. That is why Christ had to go to jail, and you and I may have to also.

Our sacred vocation is clear and urgent: to participate in the transformation of ourselves, our neighbor, and the world with all of its complexities. To do this we must eat. We must drink. We must feed ourselves, but not too much so that the rest of the world can also be fed. "We are in an unusual situation as a civilization," said Al Gore, "in that the maximum that is politically feasible, even the maximum that is politically imaginable right now, still falls short of the minimum that is scientifically and ecologically necessary."

The world is in danger at its heart. You may reap the harvest of God's goodness or the curse of sin committed before you were even born. I never think of evil or sin as small, but I do think of God as much larger. I am a spiritually reluctant, spiritually hesitant, spiritual amateur trying to become a spiritual animator so as to be alive myself in a spiritually vivid world. I hope you will do the same.

I kept an unsigned prayer next to my bed for a long time. It read:

> That I not be a restless ghost,
> Who haunts your footsteps as they pass,
> Beyond the point where you have left me,

Standing in the new spring breeze.
You must be free to take a path,
Whose End I feel is hard to know.

Another favorite prayer of mine, also anonymous, constitutes my benediction for you as well:

May you sing so much that you become song.
May you dance so much that you become dance.
May you love so much that you become love.

May you work as though you don't need the money.
Love as though you have never been hurt.
Dance as though no one was looking.

And Victor Hugo expressed my interfaith blessing for you the best of all:

And yet sings,
Knowing she hath wings.

Be like that Bird
Who, pausing in flight,
Feels the bough give way
Beneath her feet
And yet sings,
Knowing she hath wings.

Notes

1. See Beatrice Siegel, *The Making of a Crusader* (New York: Simon and Schuster, 1995), 120, 129.

2. Jerry Adler, "A Matter of Faith," *Newsweek,* December 15, 1997.

3. As quoted in ibid., 54.

4. Judy Petsonk and Jim Remsen, *The Intermarriage Handbook* (New York: William Morrow, 1988).

5. Ibid., 25.

6. See Mary Helene Rosenbaum, Stanley Rosenbaum, and Ned Rosenbaum, *Celebrating Our Differences: Living Two Faiths in One Marriage* (Shippensburg, Pa.: White Mane Publications, 1999).

7. Susan Schneider, *Intermarriage: The Challenge of Living with Differences between Jews and Christians* (New York: William Morrow, 1989).

8. Meryl Hyman, *Who Is a Jew? Conversations, Not Conclusions* (New York: Jewish Lights (Free Press), 1998).

9. In the chapter "Enough Jewish," in Nathan Glaser, *Strangers to the Tribe: Portraits of Interfaith Marriage* (Boston: Houghton Mifflin, 1997).

10. John Hick, "Beyond Objectivism and Relativism," in *The Problems of Religious Pluralism* (New York: St. Martin's Press, 1985), 18.

11. See Paul Cowan with Rachel Cowan, *Mixed Blessings: Overcoming the Stumbling Blocks in an Interfaith Marriage* (Penguin Books, 1987); Leslie Goodman-Malamuth and Robin Margolis, *Between Two Worlds: Choices for Grown Children of Jewish-Christian Parents* (New York: Pocket Books, 1992); Sunie Levin,

Mingled Roots: A Guide for Jewish Grandparents of Interfaith Grandchildren (B'Nai B'rith Women, 1992); Andrea King, *If I'm Jewish and You're Christian, What Are the Kids? A Parenting Guide for Interfaith Families* (New York: UAHC Press, 1994); Lee F. Gruzen, *Raising Your Jewish-Christian Child: Wise Choices for Interfaith Parents* (New York: Dodd, Mead, 1987).

12. Robert McAfee Brown, *The Spirit of Protestantism* (Oxford: Oxford University Press, 1961), 123.

13. Gregory J. Riley, *One Jesus, Many Christs: How Jesus Inspired Not One True Christianity but Many* (New York: Harper, 1997).

14. NPR interview, April 15, 1998.

15. Peter Megargee Brown, *Village: Where and How to Live* (New York: Benchmark Press, 1996).

16. A good introduction to the enneagram is available in Rabbi Howard A. Addison, *The Enneagram and the Kabbalah* (New York: Jewish Lights, 1998). It examines what the enneagram's nine-pointed star and the Sefirot of Kabbalah's Tree of Life have in common. One comes from ancient Sufi tradition and the other from ancient Jewish tradition. It is astonishing how similar the personality types are. Each has a theory of polarity, showing that in great virtue there is great vice and proving once and for all that we can see what we can see only from where we are sitting. We can't see much beyond. If the Myers-Briggs scale of personalities as either intuitive or rational, perceptive or judging, has been an aid to you in your home or office, getting hold of these mystical psychologies can help you see the diversity of religious perspectives. They also show why Venus is often so far away from Mars, and why there are some people you just do not understand. Another good resource is Jerome Wagner, *The Enneagram Spectrum of Personality Styles* (Portland, Ore.: Metamorphous Press, 1996). The first text written on the enneagram from a Jewish perspective is Miriam Adahan's *Awareness* (New York: Feldheim, 1994). Another good introduction is Richard Rohr, *Discovering the Enneagram* (New York: Crossroad, 1992). These spiritual tools date from the fifth century C.E. They tell us that diversity of religious access has been around for a long, long time.

17. Kim Chernin, *In My Father's Garden: A Daughter's Search for a Spiritual Life* (Chapel Hill, N.C.: Algonquin Books, 1996).

18. Catherine L. Albanese, "Exchanging Selves, Exchanging Souls," in *Retelling U.S. Religious History,* ed. Thomas Tweed (Berkeley: University of California Press, 1997), 224.

19. Ibid., 223.

20. Lecture, Minneapolis, November 1998.

21. Petsonk and Remsen, *The Intermarriage Handbook.*

22. Robert Bellah et al., *Habits of the Heart* (Berkeley: University of California Press, 1985), 221, 235.

23. Walter Brueggemann understands subversion as "flying low under the dominant version with a subversive offer of another version to be embraced by subversives....We are indeed a sub people ...sub-versive, sub-verted, sub-verting, sub-rosa, and sub-tle. We are on the ground, underneath official versions....The dominant version is violence" ("Preaching a Sub-Version," *Theology Today,* July 1998, 200, 212).

24. Leslie Goodman-Malamuth and Robin Margolis, *Between Two Worlds: Choices for Grown Children of Jewish-Christian Parents* (New York: Pocket Books, 1992).

25. Sunie Levin, *Mingled Roots: A Guide for Jewish Grandparents of Interfaith Grandchildren* (B'Nai B'rith Women, 1992).

26. Sue Hubbell, *A Country Year: Living the Questions* (New York: Random House, 1986).

27. Carole Klein, *Mothers and Sons* (Boston: Houghton Mifflin, 1984).

28. Mimi Doe with Marsha Walch, *Ten Principles for Spiritual Parenting* (San Francisco: Harper Perennial, 1998).

29. See Erik Erikson for a good listing of the stages.

30. Roy Blount, Jr., *Be Sweet: A Conditional Love Story* (New York: Alfred A. Knopf, 1998), 9.

31. Joan Hawxhurst, *The Interfaith Family Guidebook: Practical Advice for Jewish and Christian Partners* (Kalamazoo, Mich.: Dovetail Publishing, 1998.)

32. Abraham Joshua Heschel, *Moral Grandeur and Spiritual Audacity,* ed. Susannah Heschel (New York: Farrar, Straus & Giroux, 1996), 21.

33. Barbara Dafoe Whitehead, *The Divorce Culture* (New York: Alfred A. Knopf, 1997), 45.

34. Mary Pipher, *The Shelter of Each Other: Rebuilding Our Families* (New York: Grosset Putnam, 1997).

35. Ibid., 31.

36. See Jeremy Rifkin, *The End of Work* (New York: G. P. Putnam's Sons, 1995) for a way to get to the four-hour day.

37. Nick Stinnett and John De Frain, *The Secrets of Strong Families* (Boston: Little, Brown, 1985).

38. Pipher, *The Shelter of Each Other,* 149.

39. Trin Min Ha, *Rethinking Borders,* ed. John C. Welchman (Minneapolis: University of Minnesota Press, 1996).

40. Available through LOGOS at 1-800-328-0200.

41. Heschel, "No Religion Is an Island," in *Moral Grandeur and Spiritual Audacity,* 241.

42. Kathleen Norris, *Amazing Grace: A Vocabulary of Faith* (New York: Riverhead Books, 1998).

43. Harriet Lerner, *The Dance of Intimacy* (New York: Harper and Row, 1989).

44. Virginia Owens, *Selling Jesus in the Modern Age* (Grand Rapids, Mich.: Eerdmans, 1971), 8.

45. Ibid., 64.

46. Ibid., 124.

47. Mark Slouka, *War of the Worlds: Cyberspace and the High-tech Assault on Reality* (Basic Books), quoted in *Harper's,* August 1995, 36ff.

48. Kevin Kelley, *Out of Control: The Rise of Neo-Biological Civilization* (Reading, Mass.: Addison-Wesley, 1994).

49. Janet Horowitz Murray, *Hamlet of the Holodeck: The Future of Narrative in Cyberspace* (New York: Free Press, 1997).

50. William James, *The Varieties of Religious Experience* (New York: Basic Books, 1985), 350.

51. Bernie Glassman, in *Tikkun* 13, no. 1 (January–February 1998).

52. Walter Brueggemann, *Texts under Negotiation* (Minneapolis: Fortress Press, 1993).

53. Frederick Franck, "The Artist-Within and the Contemplative Eye," *Image,* September 1995, 28.

54. Heschel, *Moral Grandeur and Spiritual Audacity,* 237.

55. Abraham Joshua Heschel, quoted in Robert Ellsberg, *All Saints: Daily Reflections on Saints, Prophets, and Witnesses for Our Time* (New York: Crossroad, 1997), 241.

56. Kathleen Norris, *Amazing Grace: A Vocabulary of Faith* (New York: Riverhead Books, 1998), 232.